Creating Your Own Future

A Woman's Guide to Retirement Planning

BY JUDITH A. MARTINDALE
AND MARY J. MOSES

SOURCEBOOKS TRADE
NAPERVILLE, ILLINOIS

Sourcebooks Trade
A Division of Sourcebooks, Inc.
P.O. Box 372
Naperville, Illinois, 60566
(708) 961-2161

ISBN: 0-942061-08--X (hardcover); 0-942061-09-8 (paperback)

Editorial: Ellen Slezak
Design and Production: Monica Paxson
Proofreading: Joyce Petersen
Indexing: Lynn Brown

In cooperation with the Partners in Publishing Program

 KENDALL/HUNT PUBLISHING COMPANY
2460 Kerper Boulevard P.O. Box 539 Dubuque, Iowa 52004-0539

0-8403-6437-7 (hardcover); 0-8403-6429-6 (paper)

This publication is designed to provide accurate and authoritative information in regard to the subject matter covered. It is sold with the understanding that the publisher is not engaged in rendering legal, accounting, or other professional service. If legal advice or other expert assistance is required, the services of a competent professional person should be sought.

From a Declaration of Principles Jointly Adopted by a Committee of the American Bar Association and a Committee of Publishers and Associations

---

Library of Congress Cataloging-in-Publication Data

Martindale, Judith A., 1947-
        Creating your own future : a woman's guide to retirement planning
by Judith A. Martindale and Mary J. Moses.
        p.   cm.
        Includes bibliographical references and index.
        ISBN 0-942061-08-X (hardcover) -- ISBN 0-942061-09-8 (pbk.)
        1. Women--United States--Retirement. 2. Retirement--United
    States--Planning.   I. Moses, Mary., J., 1928- . II. Title.
HQ1063.2.U6M3   1991
646.7'9'082--dc20   **053399**   90-46484
                                                                    CIP

---

10 9 8 7 6 5 4 3 2

Table of Contents

Creating Your Own Future

Acknowledgments

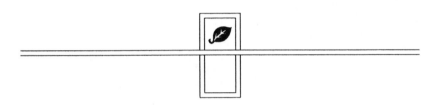

Our thanks go to the women and men who helped with this project. Many of the retired women whom we interviewed asked to remain anonymous, and we honor their wishes, but they have the personal satisfaction of knowing that their contributions have helped many other women.

Special thanks from Mary Moses go to Carol McPhee Norton and Ann FitzGerald, for their enthusiasm and encouragement when the concept was as yet not put into words; Lillian Dean, for sharing all my writer's insecurities; Terry and Lewis Shireman and their families, for shouting, "Yea, Mom" and "You can do it!" at all the right times; Pam and Mike Askew, Ruby Waldhelm, Pat Angel, and Dorothy and Estel Beath, for knowing and understanding even when I didn't; Charmaine O'Hagan, Barbara Mannetter, Sandee Hastings, and other office staff who endured my jitters and far-away looks; and Judi Martindale, for teaching me so much.

Creating Your Own Future

Special thanks from Judi Martindale go to Lillian Dean, for bringing Mary and me together in our first teaching assignment; Vickie Bookless, for keeping my spirits high; Dr. Nathaniel and Devers Branden and Barbara Scott, for their emotional guidance and support; Jan Calcaterra, for her unending willingness to type and add "just a few more changes"; and my clients who have trusted me with their stories, their dreams, and their money.

From both of us: We are grateful to Dominique Raccah and her staff for their faith and trust in us, and especially for their patience with our shortcomings. A large "Thank you and good luck" to the women who have taken our classes and from whom we have learned so much.

Judith Martindale and Mary Moses

Introduction

Preparation of this book was an educational experience for the authors. We had been team-teaching adults for several years on subjects related to supervising employees or starting a new business. Our students were mainly women who were moving up in their careers, but who had nowhere to turn to receive this type of training. Individually we also were teaching classes. (Judi was covering financial matters, such as *Dollars and Divorce,* and Mary was teaching personnel techniques, such as *Management Skills for Secretaries*.)

Our backgrounds were diverse, but we shared a common desire to be writing a major project. Initially, the proper subject remained elusive, but we found our subject when Mary began research at the university library to better plan her retirement. She found many comprehensive books—but they were all written for men, usually by men. Occasionally, a chapter might be included that referred to "what women may want."

Creating Your Own Future

The research and study phase of our work began. We included interviews with women who were already retired.

The retirees were asked four questions:

- What was your greatest surprise in your retirement?
- What was your greatest disappointment in your retirement?
- How did you plan for your retirement?
- What advice would you give to younger women about retirement?

Women were interviewed singly and in groups, at home and at conventions, with their husbands and alone. They were enthusiastic and supportive, an example of networking at its finest. You will find the interviews scattered throughout the book, sometimes illuminating a particular point we are making, other times simply adding another voice to the medley.

When we had an outline of our material, we began giving seminars on the subject. Enrollment in our classes came as a surprise. We expected women aged 35 to 50 to respond. Instead, the ages of students ranged from women in their early 20s to those in their 80s. Women, all ages of women, wanted to know how to plan and create their future.

Eventually, we had enough material to offer an "advanced" workshop. One woman, Rosa, who had come to the first class offered, also came to the second. She was vivacious and dynamic—she stood out each time. At the beginning of each seminar, we told a great deal about ourselves to establish trust and a high comfort level for self-revelation. At the second class, Mary said, "Well, Rosa, what have you been doing since we saw you last?"

"Well," she began with a distinctive lilt to her voice, "I bought a bright red sports car. And on my 76th birthday, I learned how to ski!"

Rosa became a wonderful role model for the class. Everyone benefited from her enthusiasm for life and her savvy financial planning. By the way, Rosa is her real name, the last one you will see in this material. Names and circumstances have been changed to preserve privacy. The main elements of the women's stories are described in their voices, either in the interviews or in the anecdotal material that is woven into the text.

In addition to the interviews, you will find other elements that are repeated throughout the book. At the end of each chapter, we have included a planning chart that relates to the material covered in that particular chapter. The chart is broken down into steps you should take at different times in your life. Some entries will be the same for all age groups, others will differ. You should feel free to add items that are appropriate for you.

We also have used a format throughout the book that we have labeled *Rules* and *Easy Action Steps*. This allowed us to break the material down into digestible bites—helping you to start planning by offering tangible and *realistic* steps that you can take now.

You will find that in many chapters we have made use of an exercise called the *sentence stem technique* (explained in detail in Chapter 1) to help you expand your options.

Throughout the book, we also have listed addresses and phone numbers for many organizations and have noted books and periodicals that should be helpful to you as you begin and then continue your plan. You will also find these organizations and publications, as well as additional support sources, listed at the end of the book in the resource guide.

It has been said that writers and teachers must, to be effective, have a passion for their subject. We hope our passion inspires you to take the first steps toward creating your own future through careful and practical retirement planning.

Planning for Your Retirement—
What Lies Ahead?

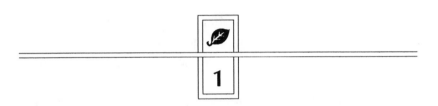

1

Every woman has the power to create her own future. With proper planning and choices, she can realize objectives and goals she never dreamed possible. You can be that woman.

Developing your potential includes meeting diverse challenges that will bring recognition for talents and skills unknown to you today. You can begin the process in easy steps, at various levels, and achieve your ideal in later years. Many women fear poverty in their old age, but careful attention to the elements of finance, health, and networking will help to negate that threat. The most important first step is the decision to take action. Apathy neither solves problems nor brings a secure future.

People often spend more time planning for an annual vacation than they do for retirement. Most people have no idea of what to expect when they retire, and they are only vaguely aware that retirement should occur sometime in their 60s. Actually, there is no mandatory retirement age, as specified in 1986 Federal legislation. *You* must decide when is the best or most appropriate time to retire.

Creating Your Own Future

Retirement planning is important for everyone, but factors unique to women make suitable preparations essential. Consider these points about women: They

- earn less than men, so the total amount available for retirement funding is less.

- tend to work for smaller organizations where no pension plan is provided. Part-time work complicates their ability to save. One American in three, about 36 million workers, works part-time, or as a temporary or contract employee. During the 1980s, this figure grew by 40 percent.[1]

- live longer. If a woman hasn't planned well, she might outlive her income and suffer a severely lowered standard of living in later years.

- take time off from the job for child care, resulting in fewer total years to contribute to a retirement plan.

- have different health needs. Older women tend to have chronic ailments, whereas the typical health problem of men is heart attack.

People look forward to calling their time their own during retirement. To turn that dream into a comfortable reality, critical decisions must be made when they are younger.

A few areas to consider are

- money
- healthcare
- housing arrangements
- use of time
- continued employment
- pension fund options
- relationships with family and friends
- Social Security materials

Some individuals are so overwhelmed by the idea that they never begin to think seriously about retirement, and trust blind luck that things will work out. Others concentrate only on financial arrangements, and give no thought to how they will use their time or where they will live.

Healthcare is a serious issue. The cost of healthcare is rising much faster than the rate of inflation. When the employer pays most or all of the cost of health insurance, apathy is an obvious result. As the cost of premiums increases, however, many employers are forced to limit coverage. Some health plans extend into retirement, some do not. The most expensive alternative is buying private health insurance on an individual basis.

Review your health insurance *before* you need it. A careful inspection of your present plan is an important step in your retirement plan. Some of the features you should know are

- the amount of the deductible.
- any illnesses or conditions excluded.
- the length of hospital stay allowed.
- outpatient services included.
- the degree of freedom you have to choose facilities and physicians.

Many believe Social Security will provide a sound financial base, becoming the foundation for peace of mind during retirement. They forget that Social Security was designed as supplemental income, not as a substitute for savings.

A woman may believe her own Social Security account is unimportant because she expects to claim retirement benefits as her husband's dependent. A dependent wife receives 50 percent of her husband's benefit under Social Security when he is retired and when she reaches age 65, or 38 percent of his benefit when she reaches age 62. If this is her only source of income, she will face severe financial constraints. If she has worked outside the home, she may be better off claiming retirement benefits under her own account, rather than as a dependent wife.

Social Security provides survivors' benefits for the widowed, for dependent children under age 18, and for disabled persons of all ages. The widow's benefit is available through Social Security when she reaches age 60. In the United States, the average age a woman becomes widowed is 56.

A worker may continue to earn some wages after beginning Social Security retirement income, provided an annual exempt amount is not exceeded. Continued employment after formal retirement is an attractive choice because it:

- gives the worker an identity.
- provides additional income.
- supplies necessary social contacts.
- satisfies the need to contribute to the community and to society.

Part-time work allows the retired person the best of two worlds: free time to enjoy leisure activities, as well as the benefits of employment. Do not count it out as an option. New labor markets are opening to older workers as the barriers of age discrimination are coming down. Many states have laws and penalties regarding age bias.

A frequent response to financial or overall planning is, "I have so little, why bother?" The answer is, "You probably have more than you realize." Fear of admitting poor choices causes some people to resist an evaluation of their financial position. They become alarmed when they realize how much they spend on consumable items and impulse purchases, or how much they owe on credit cards.

Reduced expenditures means more money is available to save. The same is true of reduced debt. If you can maintain a current balance on credit cards, for example, it will be easier for you to put money into savings for retirement. No matter how small the amount, a regular savings plan has the combined benefits of creating a good financial habit for the individual while the interest compounds and boosts the principal.

The best ways to save are

- Make savings a TOP priority.

- Start now with regular amounts, no matter how small.
- Take advantage of "painless" methods of deposit.
- Reduce debt.
- Review past decisions and spending habits to find new sources of cash.

The purpose of planning is to provide for retirement *living expenses*. You can assess the retirement lifestyle you're likely to want from the decisions you've made to date. An appropriate retirement lifestyle may be developed from today's decisions.

Careful consideration of after-retirement activities will substantially influence your financial base requirements. One couple may dream of travel in a motor home, whereas another may choose to help disadvantaged people through church work. One woman may take advantage of the opportunity to learn to play a musical instrument, a lifelong ambition; another may become active in politics or volunteer to work with handicapped children.

Grown children who no longer require financial assistance are a thing of the past. Fewer young families are able to afford a first home on their own and many look to their parents for financial help. Often parents are paying for their children's college costs while saving for their own retirement. And because women today are generally waiting longer to have children, a couple could have children in college while caring for aged parents.

Some couples plan together for retirement through one party's pension plan. Then divorce, an unexpected factor, strips away that protection for the other person. Financial responsibility is the concern of every individual.

The best contingency is for each person—married or not—to become self-reliant. Couples should consider all possibilities when planning together, and they should aim for a state of "cooperative independence." Both parties deserve equal consideration.

Creating Your Own Future

The financial base for retirement is complex and requires much thought. The important point is to have a central place for all the crucial data that will help you make decisions. A loose-leaf notebook or binder can be helpful in making these plans. Label the sections:

- Annual net worth statement
- Family responsibilities
- Lifestyle plans
- Investments and investment strategies
- Important papers and their location
- Healthcare reminders
- Social Security updates

Let's look at the information you should include in each section of your plan.

—*Annual net worth statement.* An annual balance sheet that measures your current financial position. When conducted on a regular basis, it will provide you with a summary of financial activity at a glance.

—*Family responsibilities.* Influences on your income and expenses in later years must be considered. Is it possible that you might be the care provider for an elderly parent or in-law? Women have a traditional image of being nurturing, and it often falls on them to take charge of elderly family members, including their husbands' parents.

—*Lifestyle plans.* Use your imagination when considering the lifestyle that will bring you greatest satisfaction and happiness in later years. You should develop a clear concept of how you expect to live after retirement. The bumpersticker that reads "Retirement Means Half as Much Money and Twice as Much Husband" contains a kernel of truth.

Take the example of Verna L., who retired from the working world when her husband did, she from teaching, he from industry. Retirement occurred earlier than they wished because the company he worked for was swallowed up in a corporate takeover, and he, along with many others, was asked to take early retirement. His retirement income was less than they had hoped, but in addition to Verna's, it was adequate.

Verna rejoined the work force part-time as the public relations director for a large hospital. The balance of her time was spent in community activities. She quickly rose to the governing boards of the organizations in which she was active.

After several years, Verna asked herself if she should quit her part-time job. She did not want to work past the point of producing top-quality work, as she had seen some older workers do. Her husband assured her that they could get by on their retirement incomes. The critical issue for her was: Am I willing to do what I am doing now for pay at the hospital for free as a volunteer? Her answer: Not yet. She knew she would be thinking of the missing paycheck, and would resent the requests of volunteer groups. She decided to reevaluate on an annual basis.

If you are outgoing and active, like Verna, and select a retirement lifestyle that requires financial support—dues, transportation, refreshments, appropriate wardrobe, and cash contributions—include these essentials in your design. Also consider that you might be interested in learning new skills—say, golf or tennis. Sports equipment, lessons, and playing fees would be new expenses.

—*Investments and Investment Strategies.* This section should receive a great deal of attention. Strategies are the channels through which your investment goals will be achieved. Generally, the younger the investor, the less disposable income she will have to invest. Her emphasis should be on appreciation, or growth. The older investor who is within sight of retirement will find income, or yield, of greater importance. The time factor influences both women.

Expect your plan and investments to change over time. Some portions may move more quickly than others. The advantage of this section of your notebook is the same as the net worth statement—the data are all in one place. Make it a habit to place the regular mutual funds or transaction reports from your financial planner in your planning binder.

Two women were talking quietly in a coffee shop. Ethel's low-key manner had brought a sense of equilibrium to the elementary school office where she had spent most of her career. She and her husband were now enjoying retirement—almost.

Ethel, the elder of the two, was a quiet contrast to June, who was vivacious and animated. June and her husband were also retired. Ethel was thoughtful and shy, June quick and outgoing. June had always been a homemaker, but had given a career's worth of time to voluntary public service. Her two sons were out of college and on their own at last, so she and her husband were enjoying retirement.

Ethel spoke softly, "The biggest adjustment I had to make was living with a husband 24 hours a day. I found a new and different man in my husband. I got to know him at a personal level. I learned why he reacts the way he does. Children can be an adjustment, too. If you're at a loss for outside interests, you tend to dwell on your children and their lives. You want them to be too dependent on you. I was doing that, but I finally realized what I was doing to them and to myself."

"I don't think a retired woman should be the resident babysitter, either," June responded. "She should set up a schedule when she can be available to sit for her grandchildren, but she should have time for herself, too.

"I also believe you are not financially responsible for your grown children. Any financial dealings should be done on a businesslike basis. Pretend you are lending money to someone you don't like."

Ethel nodded, "Another thing is that when you are 35 or 40, you should choose a well-being program. When you retire, you need it more than ever. It should suit you. I love my aqua-exercise class. I especially enjoy walking because I can be alone. It's my time to myself."

"Me, too," said June, "I get the best solutions to prob-
lems when I'm running. You also need to develop
support groups. It's hard to overestimate the positive
role a church plays in developing support groups. Or develop an interest in
music, cards, or art. But a woman shouldn't wait until she's retired to start
those things. Support groups are great, no matter if you're a couple or if
you're alone."

"Getting my husband to go anywhere is tough," Ethel admitted.

"I had the same problem, but I just made it a point to schedule things he
would like to do, and I included other people. At first he balked, but I ignored
it and did it anyway. Now, he's much better. Start small and keep at it."

"I will," Ethel smiled.

June went on, "I learned something related to this subject when I
visited relatives this summer. I learned to my surprise that it isn't just the
girls in the family who are interested in getting the china, or the family
photos, or the jewelry. We sometimes overlook the boys, or assume they
aren't interested.

"I also got a good idea from a financial consultant. She said a duplex
is a good living arrangement for a single woman. It brings in an income,
which helps pay for itself, and it keeps someone close by."

"That's a support system right there," Ethel added.

"Yes, and I met a widow, whose house is free and clear, but who pays
herself rent every month. She sets that money aside for maintenance, so
there's always a nest egg for those unexpected repairs that always seem to
crop up."

"One more thing that's important," Ethel concluded, "is being of
service to somebody else, outside the family, I mean. It's a great way to meet
others, and there's a big satisfaction internally. It keeps you young."

—*Important papers and their location.* You may know exactly where all your valuable papers are at the present time, but certain provisions should be made so that another person could reach them at your direction. A listing in your notebook will also remind you of renewals or updating that needs to be done on a regular basis.

—*Healthcare reminders.* Scheduling of regular healthcare examinations and the subsequent test results should be put here. Some physicians advise their patients to keep test results and to take them along when traveling, so that if you get sick, the local doctor has immediate data to go on.

—*Social Security updates.* Social Security data will play an important role in your retirement, not only for income but also for access to Medicare and related benefits. Keep all your records in a central location or identify clearly where they may be found.

Your financial planning notebook will give you the satisfaction of watching your assets accumulate, and you will also find it helpful each year when you're preparing your income taxes.

After your savings begin to accumulate, you should study more sophisticated and rewarding methods of handling money. The old adage "don't put all your eggs in one basket" applies to your nest egg. Books, magazines, and newsletters are available as resources. Public libraries are excellent support systems to help you investigate all types of investments, as well as specific companies.

You should monitor your health problems, both real and potential, as closely as you do your financial situation. It is easy to assume that you will always be in the same state of health as you are today, but that is not the case for many women. For example, if a certain disease or condition is prevalent in a woman's family, she should read about the condition, and ask questions of her physician. They should both be alert to signals of the disease. Preventative measures and regular examinations are a must.

The older woman is likely to be alone. Statistically, men live fewer years than women, yet many women are not willing to face that possibility. Some say, "If I am widowed, I will marry again," but older women are less apt to remarry, simply because there are fewer single men. In 1980 slightly more than 10 percent of the total population of the United States was age 65 or older, about 25.5 million. About 15 million of these people were women and 10 million were men.[2] This gender gap widens as people age.

In 1975, there were about seven men for every 10 women between the ages of 65 and 74. In the next age decade (74 to 84), there were only six men for every 10 women.[3] About 75 percent of men age 65 and over were married.[4] Or, to view the same problem from another perspective, in 1970 only 3 out of every 1000 brides were age 65 or older.[5]

Appraisal of acceptable single lifestyles also is important. Many older women are content living alone, happy to make spur-of-the-moment decisions without consulting anyone. Others long for the companionship and conversation of a partner. One person may be delighted with sharing her house with another, while the next may feel crowded and inconvenienced. Much thought and consideration must be given to these options—these are decisions that should not be made in haste or under pressure.

Internal blocks may prevent success in relationships and in activities. How many times have you heard someone say, with envy, "That's wonderful, but I could never do that"? You may be sure that she can accomplish the task, but she will not allow herself to accept responsibility for the activity. Or perhaps you have heard another version of the same lament, one that goes, "Oh, I'm just a secretary," or account executive, or whatever. These examples indicate an important internal block: neither woman gives herself permission to be successful.

Dr. Nathaniel Branden, a psychologist in Los Angeles, has originated and developed a wide variety of uses for the sentence completion process that we have adapted in principle here. Use each beginning, or sentence stem, provided. Quickly, and without censorship, add 10 endings to each sentence. Do not edit in any way. When you believe you cannot think of another response, invent an ending, no matter how unrelated. You can say your endings aloud, write them down, or save them in a tape recorder. The process enables you to explore your thoughts and feelings and will often tap into important emotional sources. The technique has almost universal application.

Try finishing these stems:

- Success to me means. . .
- If Mother saw me succeeding, she would. . .
- If Father saw me succeeding, he would. . .
- The good thing about stopping short is. . .
- If I didn't stop myself, I could. . .

Success for the individual depends not so much on pure skill as on self-confidence, which is the direct result of self-empowerment. You can release this energy by internally allowing yourself to accept the power given you from external sources.

If you find it difficult to accept external power, overcome this reluctance by practicing in small, easy increments. For example, if someone compliments you on your dress, smile and say, "Thank you. I am glad you like it," rather than saying "Oh, this old thing" (or some variant that downgrades both your choice and their opinion). With the former, you give the other person the power to compliment you and to express her opinion, and you empower yourself to make more successful choices in the future. Didn't she confirm your good taste?

Self-generated power is also the knowledge that you can do anything you want to do. To women in Western culture, power sometimes has a negative reputation and is associated with ruthless aggression. Actually, power is more closely related to influence or the ability to produce an effect or action and is a component of motivation. The strength gained from self-empowerment can help transform your thoughts and ideas into activity directed toward your goals.

Self-empowerment can be an important tool in finding appropriate solutions to conflicting circumstances. Research among the older population reveals data of a dual nature. First, people find great satisfaction in old age because they see the fruition of all their plans and dreams. They can stand back and admire their accomplishments and, at the same time, continue to create and contribute. On the other hand, a pattern of problems emerges in old age, including a reduction of income, changes in social roles, and various health problems.[6] Self-empowerment and awareness of these issues can help you develop the best solutions for you.

Retirement can be the beginning of a new dimension to life. When no longer confined to the structure of a daily job, a person is free to explore the surrounding world. The quality of that period of life will depend, in a large part, on planning.

Endnotes

1. "Executive Fitness" Rodale Press (April 1989), Vol. 20, No. 4, p. 4.

2. U.S. Senate, Special Committee on Aging. *Developments in Aging. 1981* (Washington, DC: GPO, 1982), Vol. 1, Senate Report 97-314.

3. Rubinstein, Robert L. *Singular Paths: Old Men Living Alone.* (New York: Columbia University Press), 1986, p.2.

4. Brody, E. M. "Women in the middle," *Gerontologist*, 1981, Vol. 21, pp. 471-480.

5. Trease, J., and Van Helst, A. "Marriage and remarriage rates among older Americans," *Gerontologist*, 1976, Vol. 16, pp. 132-136.

6. Rubinstein, op. cit., p. 15.

Planning Chart—Chapter 1

Your age now:

20s	30s	40s	50s
Begin a notebook	Begin notebook, if not done already	Continue notebook	Same
Self-esteem enhance-ment and evaluation	Same	Same	Same
Start saving regularly	Start investment program	Diversify investments	Reevaluate
Establish credit	Monitor credit	Same	Same
Set up emergency fund	Adjust fund to income	Same	Same
Adequate insurance	Same	Evaluate insurance	Reevaluate insurance
	Begin saving for children's education	Redirect to retirement	Same
	Begin retirement planning	Continuous	Continuous

Is Social Security Enough?

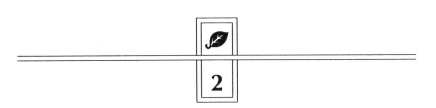

2

Social Security is the largest public program of its type in the United States, and women make up a major part of that benefit system. Out of the 24.5 million beneficiaries aged 65 or older in 1976, 59 percent were women. Nearly twice as many women receive benefits as the wives of workers than as workers in their own right. Retired women receive substantially less in dollar revenues under Social Security than men.[1]

The Social Security system incorporates a series of three financial protections—retirement income, disability insurance, and survivors' benefits—that have almost universal application within the United States.

Retirement income benefits are available to workers who have earned credit within the system for a certain amount of work. One Social Security credit is frequently called *one quarter of coverage*. All credits are earned in the same manner: by the amount of annual earnings. In

1988, one credit was granted for each $470 of annual earnings, up to a maximum of four, based on annual earnings of $1,880 or more, for gross wages and net self-employment income. After that date, the amount needed to earn one credit is scheduled to increase automatically as average wages increase.

Most, but not all, jobs in the United States are covered by Social Security, and some have special rules that apply. Included in these special categories are

- Domestic services
- Farm workers
- Nonprofit organization employees
- Federal employees
- Work done by family members
- Members of the military
- Self-employed persons

If you fall within these groups now, or have done so in the past, contact your nearest Social Security office for specific details of your coverage. All offices are listed in the telephone book white pages under: United States Government Offices, Department of Health and Human Services, Social Security Administration.

If you stop working outside the home, your account will remain available for adding more credits when you return to work. However, no benefits based on your earnings can be paid to you or your dependents until you have the minimum number of credits.

The minimum number of credits needed to be fully insured is 40 for workers at age 62 in 1991 or later. Note: Having the basic number of credits in your account only means you are *eligible* for certain benefits; it has no bearing on the amount. The amount of your retirement benefit from Social Security is determined by your earnings over a certain number of years, depending on the year you reach age 62. All your earnings up to the maximum allowed are considered.

Exhibit 2-1 should be considered for estimates only. Many variables can alter the amount you will receive. Keep careful records, and as you near retirement time, visit your local Social Security office for more accurate details.

Most people think of retirement at age 65, but under Social Security rules, only persons who were born in 1937 or earlier qualify for full benefits at age 65. Under present provisions, a woman born in 1938 will not receive full benefits until she retires at age 65 years and 2 months, and a worker born after 1960 must wait to age 67 to retire with full Social Security benefits.

To calculate the year you will be eligible for full Social Security retirement benefits, jot down the following:

- From Exhibit 2–2, based on your year of birth, indicate when you will qualify $\underline{\hspace{2cm}}$ $\underline{\hspace{2cm}}$

                                            yr   mo

- Subtract your present age $-\underline{\hspace{2cm}}$

- Answer is number of years to go $=\underline{\hspace{2cm}}$

- Now, add the current year (e.g., 1991) to the number of years to go $+\underline{\hspace{2cm}}$

- The sum of the last two gives you the year you will qualify $=\underline{\hspace{2cm}}$

A worker can retire early, as soon as age 62, but her retirement benefits will be reduced *permanently*, to compensate for the longer period she is expected to draw benefits. Thus, if she elects to retire before the age when she is entitled to full benefits, she will receive a reduced amount, and that amount *will not* be adjusted when she reaches the age accorded full benefits.

Reduction Table

At age 62, benefits will be reduced by 20 percent

At age 63, benefits will be reduced by 13 percent

At age 64, benefits will be reduced by 6.5 percent

Exhibit 2-1

The following table shows benefits payable to the worker and spouse. To use the table, find your age and the earnings closest to your earnings in 1987. These figures will give you an estimate of the amount of your retirement benefits at various ages.

Approximate monthly retirement benefits if the worker retires at normal retirement age and had steady lifetime earnings

Worker's Age in 1988	Worker's Family	Retired Worker's Earnings in 1987						
		$10,000	$15,000	$20,000	$25,000	$30,000	$35,000	$43,800 or More
25	Retired worker only	$618	$801	$983	$1,129	$1,214	$1,300	$1,471
	Worker and spouse	927	1,201	1,474	1,693	1,821	1,950	2,206
35	Retired worker only	572	740	908	1,045	1,123	1,203	1,358
	Worker and spouse	858	1,110	1,362	1,567	1,684	1,804	2,037
45	Retired worker only	523	677	831	958	1,030	1,092	1,201
	Worker and spouse	784	1,015	1,246	1,437	1,545	1,638	1,801
55	Retired worker only	475	614	754	862	910	946	1,003
	Worker and spouse	712	921	1,131	1,293	1.365	1,419	1,504
65	Retired worker only	425	550	675	768	797	816	838
	Worker and spouse	637	825	1,012	1,152	1,195	1,224	1,257

Note: Spouse is assumed to be the same age as the worker. Spouse may qualify for a higher retirement benefit based on his or her work record. The accuracy of these estimates depends on the pattern of the worker's actual past earnings and on his or her earnings in the future.

Exhibit 2–2

Year of birth	Normal retirement age
1937 or earlier	65
1938	65 and 2 months
1939	65 and 4 months
1940	65 and 6 months
1941	65 and 8 months
1942	65 and 10 months
1943–1954	66
1955	66 and 2 months
1956	66 and 4 months
1957	66 and 6 months
1958	66 and 8 months
1959	66 and 10 months
1960 and later	67

Normal retirement age is the earliest age at which unreduced retirement benefits can be reserved.

For some, the early retirement selection is a better choice. The staff at the Social Security office, or the printout you receive upon requesting your account status, will show you an estimated amount with retirement at full benefits. Use your calculator to determine the dollar amount of the reduction. Then calculate how long it would take you to reach the break-even point if you took the lower amount.

For example, if your estimated full benefit at age 65 would be $550 but you prefer to retire at age 62, your benefit would be 20 percent less ($440) *forever*. To understand what this means overall, make a grid as follows: In the center of a page, make two columns; label one "62" and the other "65." At the top of each column, multiply your estimated monthly benefit by 12 to give the annual amount you would receive. Along the left-hand side of the page list your age in consecutive order. At the intersections on the grid, insert the total number of dollars you will have received at the end of that year. Using the above example, the grid would look like this:

At end of age:	62	65
	$440 x 12 = $5,280	$550 x 12 = $6,600
62	5,280	0
63	10,560	0
64	15,840	0
65	21,120	6,600
66	26.400	13,200
67	31,680	19,800
68	36,960	26,400
69	42,240	33,000
70	47,520	39,600
71	52,800	46,200
72	58,080	52,800
73	63,360	59,400
74	68,340	66,000
75	73,920	72,600
76 Break-even Point	79,200	79,200
77	84,480	85,800
78	89,760	91,400

The break-even point is at the end of age 76, when the total amount received overall is equal in both columns. From that point on, the person who waits until age 65 to retire receives a greater total amount, but the person who retires at age 62 has had the advantage of income for three years, from age 62 to 65.

If a homemaker's spouse has retired, she may feel pressured into taking the reduced retirement benefit at age 62. This often happens when a woman is married to a man older than herself. She should carefully determine what her income would be if he were not there before she chooses the reduced benefit.

The woman who has been locked into a low-paying job may find it financially attractive or necessary to elect the reduced retirement option at age 62, which will put further constraints upon her income in her later years when she may be unable to work. In 1988, retirement at age 62 brought a 20 percent reduction in monthly benefits. If she was born in 1960 or later, however, the amount of the reduction at age 62 will gradually increase to 30 percent. The younger you are today, the longer you will have to wait for full retirement benefits.

Rule Number 1:   Be Sure You Have Enough Credits

Review your Social Security account on a regular basis, at least every three years, to make sure your record is in good order. All charges will be shown in the most recent printed timeframe. Your nearest Social Security office has a form that looks like Exhibit 2-3.

Obtain your free copy, fill it out, and send it to the Albuquerque Data Operations Center, Social Security Administration, P.O. Box 4429, Albuquerque, NM 87196. You may telephone a toll-free number, 1-800-234-5772, to request the same form. You may also get this form by writing the Consumer Information Center, Dept. 55-SSA, Pueblo, CO 81009. In either case, ask for form SSA-7004.

Doris K. sent for her account summary. Upon reviewing her total earnings, she found the Social Security Administration's figure was much higher than her own records. When she called the Social Security office, she learned that another woman with exactly the same first name, middle initial, last name, AND Social Security number, who lived in a different part of the country, had been paying into the same account for years. A great deal of effort and time was spent straightening out their two earnings records. Although this is un-doubtedly an unusual case, it illustrates the importance of vigilance by you, the person most likely to be affected and penalized by an error.

Take steps now to ensure the minimum number of credits are in your account. If you do not have enough credits, or estimate that you may not have enough when you get to retirement age, part-time employ-ment, enough to cover the minimum earnings requirement, may be the answer. Plan now, though your first step may not be scheduled for some time to come.

Exhibit 2–3

SOCIAL SECURITY ADMINISTRATION
Request for Earnings and Benefit Estimate Statement

To receive a free statement of your earnings covered by Social Security and your estimated future benefits, all you need to do is fill out this form. Please print or type your answers. When you have completed the form, fold it and mail it to us.

1. Name shown on your Social Security card:

First _____ Middle Initial _____ Last _____

2. Your Social Security number as shown on your card:

☐☐☐ – ☐☐ – ☐☐☐☐

3. Your date of birth: Month _____ Day _____ Year _____

☐☐ – ☐☐ – ☐☐

4. Other Social Security numbers you may have used:

☐☐☐ – ☐☐ – ☐☐☐☐
☐☐☐ – ☐☐ – ☐☐☐☐

5. Your Sex: ☐ Male ☐ Female

6. Other names you have used (including a maiden name): _____

7. Show your actual earnings for last year and your estimated earnings for this year. Include only wages and/or net self-employment income subject to Social Security tax.

A. Last year's actual earnings:

$ ☐☐☐,☐☐☐.☐ ☐
Dollars only

B. This year's estimated earnings:

$ ☐☐☐,☐☐☐.☐ ☐
Dollars only

8. Show the age at which you plan to retire: _____

9. Below, show an amount which you think best represents your future average yearly earnings between now and when you plan to retire. The amount should be a yearly average, not your total future lifetime earnings. Only show earnings subject to Social Security tax.

Most people should enter the same amount as this year's estimated earnings (the amount shown in 7B). The reason for this is that we will show your retirement benefit estimate in today's dollars, but adjusted to account for average wage growth in the national economy.

However, if you expect to earn significantly more or less in the future than what you currently earn because of promotions, a job change, part-time work, or an absence from the work force, enter the amount in today's dollars that will most closely reflect your future average yearly earnings. Do not add in cost-of-living, performance, or scheduled pay increases or bonuses.

Your future average yearly earnings:

$ ☐☐☐,☐☐☐.☐ ☐
Dollars only

10. Address where you want us to send the statement:

Name _____

Street Address (Include Apt. No., P.O. Box, or Rural Route) _____

City _____ State _____ Zip Code _____

I am asking for information about my own Social Security record or the record of a person I am authorized to represent. I understand that if I deliberately request information under false pretenses I may be guilty of a federal crime and could be fined and/or imprisoned. I authorize you to send the statement of my earnings and benefit estimates to me or any representative through a contractor.

Please sign your name (Do not print)

▶ _____

Date _____ (Area Code) Daytime Telephone No. _____

ABOUT THE PRIVACY ACT
Social Security is allowed to collect the facts on this form under Section 205 of the Social Security Act. We need them to quickly identify your record and prepare the earnings statement you asked us for. Giving us these facts is voluntary. However, without them we may not be able to give you an earnings and benefit estimate statement. Neither the Social Security Administration nor its contractor will use the information for any other purpose.

SP

Rose arranged the squares of cloth on the table. Only a few more to go and the quilt-top would be done. She always had some hand work to do—she was famous among her friends for her beautiful afghans. At the church bazaar, her items always sold first. Her doll clothes were great favorites with grandmothers as gifts for lucky grandchildren.

Rose and her husband have been retired for 10 years. They owned and operated a paint store. She said, "The biggest thing about retirement is the finances. You've got to have an income, and Social Security alone just doesn't do it.

"We didn't plan anything, but we were lucky. We had the chance to buy the building where our store was located and we took it. The property had two small apartments in addition to the retail space. Since we retired, the rents have gone up 100 percent, and we haven't gouged anybody. We charge the average of other rentals in the neighborhood."

She explained that they have doubly benefited from the investment because the rental income has increased while the value of the property has appreciated. "Those same increases would not have taken place if we had put the money into the bank or bought bonds. It was scary at the time, but it was worth the risk." Then, with a smile, she added, "Before I retired, I thought how wonderful it would be to wake up in the morning and not have a thing to do. But it hasn't been that way. I'm so busy now! And I'm having a great time."

Easy Action List

- Obtain Form SSA-7004.
- Find your Social Security card or obtain a duplicate.
- Make up a file or envelope for all your Social Security information; keep it with your notebook.

You may believe the minimum number of credits is unimportant to you because you plan to claim benefits as a dependent of your husband. As noted in Chapter 1, a dependent wife, whose husband has retired and who has never worked outside the home, receives 50 percent of her husband's benefits when she reaches age 65, or 38 percent of his benefits when she reaches age 62. A woman who has worked for a short period of time, and/or had low earnings, may receive more as a dependent wife or widow. Know your position. Keep as many options open as possible, because the laws relating to Social Security are often changed.

Because a woman may claim on her own or her husband's account, she needs to know his Social Security status. Send in a card for him, too, and get a summary for both of you at least every three years.

Rule Number 2:   Social Security Alone Is Not Enough

The Social Security Act of 1935 had two primary purposes: to provide workers with *supplemental* income during retirement and to provide an incentive for older men to retire. As you can see in Exhibit 2-4, over the years many changes have taken place. The employer and employee currently each pay a tax of 7.65 percent.

Note the fine print in footnote 4 of Exhibit 2-4: the tax rates for the self-employed are 15.3 percent and 7.65 percent for the employed as of 1990.

Although the steps for estimating benefits are complex, generally speaking, the replacement of salary ranges from about 60 percent of the wages for the worker who has always worked for minimum wage to about 26 percent for the worker who has always earned the maximum amount.[3] The formula is weighted in the form of a higher

Exhibit 2–4

Effective Earnings Base and Actual Tax Rate
Tax Rate (percent)—Employer and Employee, Each

Beginning	Annual earning base	Total	OASI	DI	HI	Maximum Tax
1937	$3,000	1.0	1.0			$ 30.00
1950	3,000	1.5	1.5			45.00
1951	3,600	1.5	1.5			54.00
1954	3,600	2.0	2.0			72.00
1955	4,200	2.0	2.0			84.00
1957	4,200	2.25	2.0	0.25		94.50
1959	4,800	2.5	2.25	.25		120.00
1960	4,800	3.0	2.75	.25		144.00
1962	4,800	3.125	2.875	.25		150.00
1963	4,800	3.625	3.375	.25		174.00
1966	6,600	4.2	3.5	.35	0.35	277.20
1967	6,600	4.4	3.55	.35	.5	290.40
1968	7,800	4.4	3.325	.475	.6	343.20
1969	7,800	4.8	3.725	.475	.6	374.40
1970	7,800	4.8	3.65	.55	.6	374.40
1971	7,800	5.2	4.05	.55	.6	405.60
1972	9,000	5.2	4.05	.55	.6	468.00
1973	10,800	5.85	4.3	.55	1.0	631.80
1974	13,200	5.85	4.375	.575	.9	772.20
1975	14,100	5.85	4.375	.575	.9	824.85
1976	15,300	5.85	4.375	.575	.9	895.05
1977	16,500	5.85	4.375	.575	.9	965.25
1978	17,700	6.05	4.275	.775	1.0	1,070.85
1979	22,900	6.13	4.33	.75	1.05	1,403.77
1980	25,900	6.13	4.52	.56	1.05	1,587.67
1981	29,700	6.65	4.7	.65	1.3	1,975.05
1982	32,400	6.7	4.575	.825	1.3	2,170.80
1983	35,700	6.7	4.575	.825	1.3	2,391.90
1984	37,800	7.0[1]	5.2	.5	1.3	2,532.60
1985	39,600	7.05	5.2	.5	1.35	2,791.80
1986	42,000	7.15	5.2	.5	1.45	3,003.00
1987	43,800	7.15	5.2	.5	1.45	3,131.70
1988	45,000[3]	7.51[4]	5.53	.53	1.45	3,379.50

[1]Employees receive a one-time credit of 0.3% for 1984.
[2]Self-employed people receive credit of 2.7% for 1984, 2.3% for 1985, and 2.0% for 1986-89.
[3]Base will increase automatically in the future to keep pace with rises in average wage levels.
[4]The tax rate will increase gradually until it is 7.65% each for employees and their employers in the year 1990 and until it is 15.3% for the self-employed in 1990.

Exhibit 2–4 (cont.)

Effective Earnings Base and Actual Tax Rate
Tax Rate (percent)—Self-employed

Beginning	Annual earning base	Total	OASI	DI	HI	Maximum Tax
1937	$3,000					
1950	3,000					
1951	3,600	2.25	2.25			$ 81.00
1954	3,600	3.0	3.0			108.00
1955	4,200	3.0	3.0			126.00
1957	4,200	3.375	3.0	0.375		141.75
1959	4,800	3.75	3.375	.375		180.00
1960	4,800	4.5	4.125	.375		216.00
1962	4,800	4.7	4.325	.375		225.60
1963	4,800	5.4	5.025	.375		259.20
1966	6,600	6.15	5.275	.525	0.35	405.90
1967	6,600	6.4	5.375	.525	.5	422.40
1968	7,800	6.4	5.0875	.7125	.6	499.20
1969	7,800	6.9	5.575	.7125	.6	538.20
1970	7,800	6.9	5.475	.825	.6	538.20
1971	7,800	7.5	6.075	.825	.6	585.00
1972	9,000	7.5	6.075	.825	.6	675.00
1973	10,800	8.0	6.205	.795	1.0	864.00
1974	13,200	7.9	6.185	.815	.9	1,042.80
1975	14,100	7.9	6.185	.815	.9	1,113.90
1976	15,300	7.9	6.185	.815	.9	1,208.70
1977	16,500	7.9	6.185	.815	.9	1,303.50
1978	17,700	8.1	6.01	1.09	1.0	1,433.70
1979	22,900	8.1	6.01	1.04	1.05	1,854.90
1980	25,900	8.1	6.01	1.04	1.05	2,097.90
1981	29,700	9.3	6.7625	1.2375	1.3	2,762.10
1982	32,400	9.35	6.8125	1.2375	1.3	3,029.40
1983	35,700	9.35	7.1125	.9375	1.3	3,337.95
1984	37,800	14.0[2]	10.4	1.0	2.6	4,271.40
1985	39,600	14.1[2]	10.4	1.0	2.7	4,672.80
1986	42,000	14.3[2]	10.4	1.0	2.9	5,166.00
1987	43,800	14.3[2]	10.4	1.0	2.9	5,387.40
1988	45,000[3]	15.02[2,4]	11.06	1.06	2.9	5,859.00

[1]Employees receive a one-time credit of 0.3% for 1984.
[2]Self-employed people receive credit of 2.7% for 1984, 2.3% for 1985, and 2.0% for 1986-89.
[3]Base will increase automatically in the future to keep pace with rises in average wage levels.
[4]The tax rate will increase gradually until it is 7.65% each for employees and their employers in the year 1990 and until it is 15.3% for the self-employed in 1990.

Grace and Glenn have always been frugal, never spending a cent when they did not need to. She was a genius at "stretching a dollar" and her skill as a manager paid off for them in their later years. Glenn had a pension from the railroad, and they enjoyed life. Between her sewing projects and his gardening, her preserving and his tinkering on the car, they kept bills at a minimum, and continued to save. They allowed themselves one big trip a year and spent the rest of their time enjoying their family and each other's company.

Grace said with a frown, "I worry about my sister. My husband and I have been retired seven years, and we're OK because we saved along the way and he has a good pension. But Sara and Hank are in a different position. He always worked for small companies that had no retirement plans, and she worked in part-time jobs, which helped keep the kids fed and clothed. They always managed to get by while the kids were growing up, but I know they don't have any savings to speak of. She's been working the past few years as a sales clerk, and now, she's going to retire. All they have is Social Security. I just don't know how they're going to make it."

percentage to the low earner to compensate for the obvious inability to accumulate retirement savings. The middle-class wage earner may also have difficulty saving but receives no advantage from the formula.

If you expect to receive a pension from a job not covered by Social Security, and you do not have enough Social Security credits in your account, you have a special reason for concern. A change in the Social Security law in 1983 may apply to you and reduce the benefits you could receive under the Social Security provisions. A complex formula determines benefits. Questions regarding this situation are best answered by counselors at the Social Security office on an individual basis. When you go to your local office, be prepared to wait; these offices are often crowded. This reduction does not apply to your other pension.[4]

Under the regular retirement provisions, for each month you delay receiving retirement benefits, starting the month you reach your retirement age (as shown in Exhibit 2-2) and ending the month you reach age 70, you will receive an extra amount in benefits in your retirement check. For workers who reached 65 in 1990 or later, the credit will gradually increase until it reaches 8 percent in the year 2009.[5]

Some of your Social Security benefits may be subject to federal income tax. If your combined adjusted gross income, plus nontaxable interest income, plus half of your Social Security benefits exceed a base amount, the smaller of one-half the difference of the combined income and the base amount or one-half of the benefits will be taxable. In 1988, the base amount was $25,000 for an individual, $32,000 for a couple filing jointly, and zero for a couple filing separately if they lived together any part of the year.[6]

Rule Number 3:   Keep an Eye on Medicare

Medicare is the federal health insurance program for people aged 65 or older and for certain disabled persons. Local Social Security Administration offices accept applications for Medicare.

Hospital Insurance (Medicare Part A)
Eligibility for this part of Medicare is available to those who are

entitled to monthly Social Security. Certain others are eligible prior to age 65, such as disabled persons.

You do not have to retire to receive this protection, but you must apply, preferably about three months prior to your 65th birthday. If you receive Social Security, your hospital insurance will start automatically at age 65.

The hospital insurance may be purchased by persons who are not otherwise eligible. In 1990, the basic premium rate was $175 per month, plus the monthly medical premium of $28.60.

Medicare pays all *allowable* charges for the first 60 days of in-patient hospital care, after you pay a $592 deductible. Additional days are partially covered.

The hospital plan, Part A of Medicare, provides for skilled nursing facility care on a partial payment basis for one hundred days. It provides no coverage for custodial care in a nursing home. Hospice care is covered up to 210 days.

Medical Insurance (Medicare Part B)
The Medicare Part B medical insurance covers physicians' services throughout the United States, including surgical procedures, diagnostic tests and X-rays that are a part of your treatment, medical supplies furnished at the doctor's office, services of an office nurse, and drugs related to your treatment but that cannot be self-administered.

Outpatient services, such as an outpatient clinic of a hospital or an emergency room, are also covered. If all required conditions are met, home health visits are included, as are other services including ambulance services and radiation treatments.

Almost anyone aged 65 or older who is eligible for the hospital insurance may enroll for the medical portion of Medicare. No Social Security credits are necessary for this insurance, but the monthly premium is recalculated annually. If you are receiving Social Security benefits, you will automatically be enrolled in the medical insurance when you become entitled to the hospital insurance, unless you specifically refuse it.

Some people *must* apply for medical insurance, including those who will work past age 65, are 65 but not eligible for hospital insurance, have permanent kidney failure, live in Puerto Rico or outside the United States, or fulfill certain other conditions.

Part B medical insurance helps pay doctors' services, medical services, and supplies not covered by the hospital portion of the plan.

After the annual deductible amount ($75 in 1990) is met, approximately 80 percent of reasonable charges for covered services are paid. The key words are "reasonable" and "covered." The difference can conceivably amount to a substantial sum, another reason to actively pursue supplemental coverage. Further instructions may be found in publications issued by the Social Security Administration, which are available free at its offices.

As Congress addresses these issues and others, further changes are certain to occur. Clip articles and news stories about the benefits and any new rules. As you approach retirement, review the materials, and take a list of questions to your local Social Security office for the latest information.

Easy Action List

- Clip one news article this month about Social Security and add it to your file.
- Clip one news article about Medicare this month and add it to your file.

Medicare will not pay all healthcare costs, and notably omits areas of special concern, such as:

- continual custodial care, including help with bathing, eating, and taking medicine
- dentures and dental care

- eyeglasses
- hearing aids
- long-term care (nursing homes)
- personal comfort items
- routine checkups and related tests

Because women generally outlive men in our society, the lack of custodial care and long-term nursing home care is of critical importance. Some insurance companies are preparing policies to help cover these costs. Talk to various insurance companies and ask your agent for details.

Easy Action List

- Read one article about custodial care or nursing home care insurance policies. Do it this week.

Employers with 20 or more employees are required to offer their older employees and spouses the same health plan that is offered younger employees. If you are planning to work past age 65, and you accept your employer's health plan, Medicare will become the secondary payer. This means your employer's plan will pay first. Since Medicare may have a lower benefit level, it is possible it would pay little or nothing under certain circumstances.

If you reject the employer's plan, Medicare becomes the primary payer, and in that case, the employer is not allowed to offer you Medicare supplemental insurance after you have rejected the regular plan.

Private insurance companies frequently recommend supplemental insurance to Medicare (sometimes called Medigap). Such services should be carefully checked, especially if you have family members who are covered under your employer's plan. Certain protections under the Veterans Administration (VA), CHAMPUS, or CHAMPVA may end or substantially change when you become eligible for Medicare. Contact the VA or related agencies prior to making your final decision about Medicare enrollment.[7]

Rule Number 4:   Know if You Qualify for Other Benefits

Other benefits under the Social Security protective umbrella are

- disability insurance
- supplemental security income (SSI)
- survivors' benefits, including widows's benefits

Disability

Under Social Security, disability is related to the capacity of a person to work. One is considered disabled when a severe physical or mental impairment, or combination of impairments, prevents that individual from gainful employment for a year or more, or if death is expected. In this context, the work does not have to be the kind done prior to the onset of the disability; it means any gainful work found in the national economy. Remember, *total disability* is required. Once a recipient begins to receive benefits, she will continue as long as she is disabled and is not engaged in substantial employment. A minimum number of credits is necessary for eligibility.

Supplemental Security Income (SSI)

Many women are unaware of this valuable program and its benefits. SSI is a federal program administered by the Social Security Administration, but is funded from income taxes, not Social Security taxes.

A person 65 or older who qualifies may receive SSI; younger persons who are blind or disabled may also qualify. These criteria alone do not automatically entitle a person to SSI. The deciding factor is the applicant's property and income.

A single person who has assets valued up to $1900 and a married couple with resources up to $2850 may receive SSI checks. Some resources do not count, such as:

- home and land the home is on
- personal and houseold goods, depending on value
- car if it is used for essential transportation and is worth $4500 or less

- burial plots, including provisions for family members
- burial funds (up to $1500 each for applicant and spouse).

Some income does not count, such as:

- the first $20 per month of any income
- the first $65 per month earned from working, and half of any amount over $65
- food stamps

A single person may be able to earn up to $793 and still get an SSI check, a couple as much as $1149.

Persons who live in city or county rest homes, halfway houses, or other public institutions usually cannot receive SSI, with a few exceptions. Persons receiving SSI often are eligible for state or county assistance, and those local agencies should be contacted for further information.[8]

SSI benefits are a mainstay for many elderly women. Of the total number of recipients of SSI over 65, approximately 2 million, or 70 percent, are women, and 97 percent of those have no other income. Janice Davidson in her contribution to the book *Life After Work*, suggests that many single older women are not receiving this benefit even though they may be eligible. Only about 30 percent of the persons who are eligible actually receive this benefit. The lack of awareness of this program by older women who qualify may explain their lack of participation.[9]

Survivors' Benefits

Survivors' benefits can be paid to the family of a deceased worker, provided Social Security credits were earned. As is commonly found in Social Security rules, a sliding scale is applied. (A sample benefits scale is shown in Exhibit 2-5.)

As a general rule, older workers need more credits than younger workers, with 40 credits the maximum. A single woman with dependent children would do well to watch the number of credits she has

Exhibit 2-5

Approximate Monthly Survivors Benefits if the Worker Dies in 1989 and had Steady Earnings

Worker's Age	Worker's Family	$10,000	$15,000	$20,000	$25,000	$30,000	$35,000	$40,000	$45,000 or More[1]
					Deceased Worker's Earnings in 1988				
25	Spouse and 1 child[2]	$686	$882	$1,078	$1,274	$1,366	$1,458	$1,550	$1,656
	Spouse and 2 children[3]	716	1,071	1,298	1,488	1,596	1,703	1,813	1,933
	1 child only	343	441	539	637	683	729	775	828
	Spouse at age 60[4]	327	420	513	607	651	695	739	789
35	Spouse and 1 child[2]	680	872	1,062	1,258	1,358	1,448	1,538	1,622
	Spouse and 2 children[3]	705	1,055	1,288	1,470	1,586	1,691	1,797	1,893
	1 child only	340	436	533	629	679	724	769	811
	Spouse at age 60[4]	324	416	508	600	647	690	733	773
45	Spouse and 1 child[2]	678	870	1,062	1,256	1,346	1,406	1,454	1,490
	Spouse and 2 children[3]	703	1,052	1,285	1,466	1,572	1,642	1,698	1,741
	1 child only	339	435	531	628	673	703	727	745
	Spouse at age 60[4]	323	415	507	598	641	670	693	710
55	Spouse and 1 child[2]	678	870	1,062	1,234	1,308	1,346	1,376	1,400
	Spouse and 2 children[3]	702	1,051	1,285	1,442	1,527	1,572	1,608	1,636
	1 child only	339	435	531	617	654	673	688	700
	Spouse at age 60[4]	323	415	506	588	623	642	656	668
65	Spouse and 1 child[2]	656	844	1,032	1,200	1,262	1,296	1,326	1,348
	Spouse and 2 children[3]	684	1,023	1,244	1,402	1,474	1,515	1,549	1,575
	1 child only	328	422	516	600	631	648	663	674
	Spouse at age 60[4]	313	402	491	572	601	618	632	643

[1] Earnings equal the Social Security wage base from age 22 through 1988.
[2] Amounts shown also equal the benefits paid to two children, if no parent survives or surviving parent has substantial earnings.
[3] Equals the maximum family benefit.
[4] Amounts payable in 1989. Spouses turning 60 in the future would receive higher benefits.
Note: The accuracy of these estimates depends on the pattern of the worker's earnings in prior years.

earned. If she should die, even though she has a responsible relative who could care for her children, the money benefits might be an important factor in their well-being and comfort.

Unmarried children up to age 18 (or older, if disabled) receive benefits. A widow may receive full benefits from her husband's account at age 65, or at any age if she is caring for an entitled child. She may apply for reduced coverage as early as age 60 if not caring for a child. The benefit paid at age 60 is 71.5 percent of the full benefit. She may remarry after age 60 (50 if she is disabled) and not disturb the widow's pension she previously received.

One of the problems a woman may face when widowed is a case in which her children reach age 18 and become ineligible for survivor's benefits at a time when she is not yet old enough to qualify under her own right. Thus, a woman widowed in her 40s or 50s, and not employed outside the home, or with few job skills, may find herself in dire straits financially.

If a woman was divorced after 10 years of marriage, and her former husband dies, she is entitled to benefits; her remarriage after age 60 will not end these payments. If she was married less than 10 years before divorce, she qualifies only if she is caring for an eligible child.

In addition to monthly survivors' benefits, a one-time lump sum death payment of $255 is available to the surviving spouse who either lived in the same household as the deceased at the time of death or was entitled to survivors' benefits on the deceased's account for the month of death. One woman, who had been married for 23 years, separated from her husband. Despondent over the possibility of a divorce, he killed himself. Because they were not living under the same roof at the time of his death, she received no survivor's benefit.

Keep in mind that when a husband who is receiving Social Security benefits dies, his widow does not receive his benefit or any portion of it. She is entitled to only the widow's benefit or to monies from her own account. The widow's benefit may or may not equal his benefit, and is subject to a different set of rules. This explains much of the poverty among elderly widows; many couples mistakenly believe that she will continue to receive both benefits after he dies. Not so.

A widow's benefit may be affected by the amount of her earnings. In 1988, the annual amount of earnings free from adjustments was $6120 for widows under age 65. From age 65 through 69, the annual exempt amount was $8400, and at age 70 and above, there was no limit on the amount of earnings. The penalty for exceeding these limits is $1 for every $3 earned.

In the year 2000, the *age* at which this withholding rate applies will gradually increase as the entire retirement schedule increases. Any earnings affect only the widow's pension, not the survivors' benefits of entitled children in her care.[10]

The Social Security Act reflects the values of the time, and many of these values can be traced directly to the Elizabethan Poor Laws, with its basic tenet that if people were poor, it was their own fault.[11] This notion continues to be reinforced because it allows dependent wives and children to receive benefits only if they are attached to a "worthy," or eligible, male worker, who retired or became disabled through no fault of his own. Women who have been divorced or deserted, or whose husbands are imprisoned, remain outside the system.[12] Assistance for widows was, and still is, related to age, not need.

Social Security alone is not enough. Understanding your Social Security benefits is but one part of creating the future you want.

Endnotes

1. Davidson, Janice. "Issues of Employment and Retirement in the Lives of Women Over Age 40." In Nancy J. Osgood, ed., *Life After Work: Retirement, Leisure, Recreation and the Elderly* (New York: Praeger Publishers, 1982), p. 108.

2. Ibid., p. 109.

3. U.S. Department of Health and Human Services, Social Security Administration. "Financial Planning and Social Security," SSA Publication No. 05-10030, January 1988.

4. U.S. Department of Health and Human Services, Social Security Administration. "How Your Social Security Check Is Affected by a Pension," SSA Publication No. 05-10045, January 1987.

5. U.S. Department of Health and Human Services, Social Security Administration. "Retirement," SSA Publication No. 05-10035, January 1988, p. 13.

6. Ibid., p. 14.

7. U.S. Department of Health and Human Services, Social Security Administration. "Disability," SSA Publication No. 05-10043, January 1988.

8. U.S. Department of Health and Human Services, Social Security Administration. "SSI," SSA Publication No. 05-11000, January 1988.

9. Davidson, op. cit., p. 110.

10. U.S. Department of Health and Human Services, Social Security Administration. "Survivors," SSA Publication No. 05-10084, January 1988.

11. Quadagno, Jill S. "From poor laws to pensions: The evolution of economic support for the aged in England and America." *Milbank Fund Quarterly,* 1984, Vol. 62, No. 3: 112-153.

12. Lopata, Helen Z., and Brehm, Henry P. *Widows and Dependent Wives: From Social Problem to Federal Program* (New York: Praeger Publishers, 1986).

Planning Chart—Chapter 2

Your age now:

20s	30s	40s	50s
Send for your Social Security summary at least every three years	At least every two years	Same	Same
Watch media for articles; clip & file	Same	Same	Same
Visit Social Security office for answers to specific questions re: elderly parents or disabled person	Same	Same	Same

What Do You Have Now?
—Evaluating Your Current Financial Position

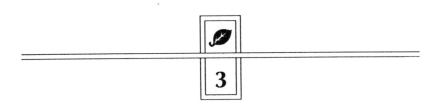

3

The first step in any financial evaluation is to examine your current position. Whether women take that first step depends upon how they feel about and react to money. Some women rarely think about money, whereas others are obsessed that they will never have enough. Most were taught that it was not a proper topic for discussion. Women were indirectly told that there was no need to plan financially because they would get married and be taken care of. The fact that some women became divorced or widowed was rarely mentioned. Consequently, women may often be ill-prepared and ill-trained to handle their finances.

Before you dive into activity with numbers, let's use the sentence stem technique to explore how you feel about money. Remember, use each beginning or stem provided, and quickly (without censorship), add 10 endings. Do not edit in any way. When you believe you cannot think of another response, invent an ending, no matter how unrelated. You will often tap into serious and important responses. Again you can say your endings into a tape recorder or write them down. The goal is to help you explore your thoughts, feelings, and relationship to money.

- Money to me means. . .
- At the thought of being responsible for my own financial future, I. . .
- When I start working with money, I. . .
- At the thought of making my own financial decisions, I. . .
- If I allowed myself to spend freely, I would. . .
- When I compare what I was promised with what I now have, I. . .
- One of the things I resent about money is. . .
- With regard to money, my parents. . .

Review your endings. Do not judge them, but be aware of your reactions. Some may surprise you. Women often say that working with money makes their eyes glaze over and their minds go blank. Persevere! This phase does not last.

To explore the concept of how women feel about carrying a lot of cash, the authors conducted an experiment during a class on financial planning. They called for a volunteer. The student, a woman, was asked to hold $1000, given to her in $100 and $50 bills. The energy and anxiety level quickly rose throughout the room. Most women were clearly uncomfortable with seeing so much cash. Only a few were blasé or indifferent. Imagine yourself in that situation and note your reaction. If you always have extra cash with you, exercise your resourcefulness and carry less as an experiment. Or leave your checkbook home for a day or a week. What are your feelings when you change your routine? These exercises not only make you more aware of your feelings about money, but can help teach you flexibility in money transactions.

The women in the class were also asked how closely they could guess the amount of money they had with them. Some women knew the exact amount, others had money wadded in several different compartments of their purses and could only roughly guess the amount they carried. Attention to detail is an indication of how seriously you treat your finances.

A net worth statement describes your current financial position. Since self-esteem is often measured in terms of money, you may find it difficult to prepare a net worth statement without feelings of success or failure. Common reactions include, "I should have done better than this by my age," and "If things are this bad, why even begin?" Although some women respond positively and are proud of their financial position, many are disappointed with their findings. You are being unfair to yourself if you measure yourself against the standards of the wealthy.

Rule Number 1:   Know Where You Are

Focus on your present situation. Examine not only your current financial condition, but also how you feel about where you are. If you reprimand yourself, it will be difficult to set goals and exercise the discipline necessary to turn them into reality. Realistic goal-setting is designed to do away with guilt.

Try these sentence stems to explore your feelings about your current financial situation:

- At the thought of organizing my finances, I. . .
- While I was organizing my balance sheet, I . . .
- At the thought of being in charge financially, I. . .
- When I look at the amount of my net worth, I. . .
- When I tell myself I should have more, I. . .

A common reaction when people are asked to compute their net worth is to make a joke about not owning enough to even bother. They use humor and self-deprecation to avoid uncomfortable feelings. Some women are pleasantly surprised when they have finished the work, because they realize they have started a process of increased financial awareness, and learn they have more than they realized. Regardless of emotional reactions, this is the place to start.

The worksheet in Exhibit 3-1 will help you compute your net worth. Feel free to add or delete categories. Revise the worksheet so it works for you.

Exhibit 3-1

Personal Financial Balance Sheet Worksheet

Assets		Liabilities	
Cash		Residence Mortgage	
Stocks		Other Mortgages	
Bonds		Loans Payable	
Loans Owed You		Current Bills Outstanding	
Residence		Other	
Retirement Plans		TOTAL LIABILITIES	
Trust Deeds			
Other Real Estate			
Limited Partnerships			
Cash Value of Life Insurance			
Personal Property			
Other			
TOTAL ASSETS		NET WORTH (Assets Minus Liabilities)	

Some people complicate this step by keeping unnecessary bank accounts throughout the country. For example, people move and never close bank accounts at their former address. Others forget items from their list of assets that would make a significant difference in the result. One couple neglected to list their airplane. Obviously, such an omission would alter the results by a substantial amount. Take your time to think about all of your assets.

After you have computed your net worth, save that information to use as a point of comparison in future years. Pick a specific day of the year when you plan to review your net worth statement and compare the gain or loss from the year before. Avoid New Year's Day, when you may be exhausted from the work of the holidays or depressed from their emotional toll. Instead, choose the weekend after your birthday or the first day of spring. You may choose to review your investment performance quarterly rather than annually, but make a commitment to evaluate your net worth at least once a year. Compare your results to your financial goals to make sure you are moving in the direction that's right for you.

The next step is to review your spending patterns. How you currently spend your money will provide the necessary information to set realistic goals. People spend money differently. Some spend every penny, whereas others are able to save regardless of their income. Jim and Sally P. wanted to plan for their retirement and for their eight-month-old daughter's college fund. Jim was a teacher, and Sally did word processing from their home. They tracked their expenses carefully and made a conscious decision to live frugally. Consequently, they were able to consider additional investments because they had more discretionary income than ever before.

Another couple was in a similar situation. Bob K. was a teacher at the same school as Jim. Patti, his wife, worked as a marketing representative and their daughter was only a few months older than Jim and Sally's child. The couples were the same age and lived in the same town. The second couple had to revise their budget to meet their expenses. They were discouraged because they had been unable to save any money. Although they worked very hard and earned a good income, they were unable to get out of a paycheck-to-paycheck mentality. In order to improve their financial condition, they had to examine and revise their spending habits.

How you handle the amount of cash you carry can provide insight into your spending patterns. Women tend to keep money in several different places in their purse. Some might keep most of their money in their wallet but also tuck a bill or two under the checkbook cover. Some women exercise the discipline to leave the extra cash alone. Others spend almost all the money they carry.

Think about the amount of cash you carry and the habits you practice. Consider handling your money differently if you are not satisfied with your current pattern. For example, if you generally spend all the money you carry, see if you can set aside a specific amount and go a week without spending it. When that exercise becomes easier, stretch the time frame to two weeks and increase the amount.

Easy Action List

- Know the exact amount of cash in your purse for a one-week period.
- Practice leaving your checkbook at home for one week.

If you find yourself overly cautious with your money, practice spending small amounts with a freer attitude. Give yourself a small present once a week—a fresh bouquet of flowers, a bar of scented soap, a facial or massage. It is easy to give to others. Try to do something just for yourself.

Few people enjoy recording how they spend money. When you begin, one of two things usually happens: either you increase your awareness of how you spend money, or you stop keeping track. Once your awareness is stimulated, certain questions must be answered and choices made. Are you willing to accept the consequences of the change you want to make? Can you make the commitment?

Rule Number 2:   Know Where Your Money Goes

Balance is the key, but the appropriate balance is different for everyone. Some spend for today and never plan for tomorrow; others save for tomorrow without enjoying life today.

Keeping track of your expenses can seem overwhelming at first, but remember, it is not a life-long activity. Try it for two or three months to discover patterns that might need to be altered. Many people resist doing this because they do not want to know how they spend their money. Staying in the dark is sometimes easier than facing reality and making hard choices. Explore how you feel about recording your expenses by completing these sentence stems—remember, push yourself until you have 10 endings.

- When I spend money, I feel. . .
- Being responsible for spending money means I must. . .
- When I control my spending, I feel. . .
- At the thought of watching every penny I spend, I. . .
- If I were to spend money differently, I would. . .

For a specific time, not less than one month, keep a paper trail of all your expenses. This is easier to do if you write checks or use credit cards and keep your cash expenditures to a minimum. At the end of the month, categorize your expenses. Exhibit 3-2 shows a sample format you can follow. If your motivation is sound but the bookwork tedious for you, hire a bookkeeper to do the paperwork for three months. Then review and evaluate your personal expenses as critically as an accountant would examine the books of a business.

Designate a specific time during the month to tabulate your spending. List the months at the top of the page, and put the expenses down the left side. Enumerate your fixed expenses first—rent or mortgage, utilities, car payments, and insurance. Next list variable expenses such as food, gas, medical, clothes, charge cards, and entertainment. The purpose of this project is to increase your awareness of how you spend money. You can use the annual expense, cash flow, and

Exhibit 3–2

Expense Tracking Chart

Date	Cost	Item	Category	Cash, Check, or Credit

Vondra smoothed her skirt across her knees and fussed with a loose thread on the cuff of her blouse. An ambulance went by, its siren filling the apartment, and making conversation impossible for a moment. She did not seem to notice the noise as she adjusted a stack of magazines on the coffee table. She had been divorced for more than twenty years, and her family lived several hundred miles away. She said, "I thought I'd do a lot of traveling after I retired, but it's so expensive. I just don't go. I find myself holding back. I have a pension from my company and my Social Security, but prices keep going up and the money stays nearly the same. I try to add to savings for a rainy day."

monthly expense worksheets provided in Exhibits 3-3, 3-4, and 3-5; purchase prepared forms from Filofax, Day Runner, Day Timer and Personal Resource Systems; or create your own.

Nancy T., although disliking the idea of keeping track of her expenses, made a two-month commitment to the assignment. She had always treated money casually but decided it was time for a change. Her biggest surprise was the amount she spent on fast-food items. As a working single parent, she was often too tired to cook and would run to the nearest fast-food restaurant instead. She was forced to weigh the convenience against the cost; she concluded some compromises were in order.

Some people are so overwhelmed with managing their money that they tolerate a constant state of chaos. Once a system is established, only a few hours a month will keep everything in order.

It will be helpful to open several different bank accounts—one for savings, one for your personal checking, and another joint checking account if you share expenses with someone. If you have a business, it is essential to establish a separate business account. Some people who open small businesses commingle their personal and business accounts because they need to "feed" the business regularly; but to ease income tax preparation and to be better prepared to handle any IRS inquiry, keep the money separate.

Before selecting a bank, review the list of services you require and then evaluate each institution accordingly. These services might include interest-bearing accounts, interstate checking, automatic teller machines, and bank-by-mail options, as well as some special services such as credit cards, traveler's checks, and safe deposit boxes. Eliminate any institution that is not covered by the Federal Deposit Insurance Corporation (FDIC) or the Federal Savings and Loan Insurance Corporation (FSLIC). The chart on page 52 gives an example of services you may want to compare.

Exhibit 3–3

Monthly Expense Worksheet

Expense Category	Monthly Total	Expense Category	Monthly Total
Home:		**Personal Grooming:**	
Rent or Mortgage	_____	Haircare	_____
Maintenance	_____	Cosmetics	_____
Property taxes	_____	Other	_____
Utilities—			
Gas, Electricity	_____	**Recreation:**	
Water	_____	Memberships	_____
Trash	_____	Vacations	_____
Telephone	_____	Subscriptions	_____
Cable	_____	Entertainment	_____
Home Furnishings	_____		
		Donations:	_____
Food:	_____		
		Gifts:	_____
Clothing:			
Purchases	_____	**Child Care:**	_____
Laundry	_____		
		Savings	_____
Transportation:			
Car payments	_____	**TOTAL**	_____
Gas	_____		
Repairs	_____		
Registration fees	_____		
Parking	_____		
Medical:			
Doctor/Dentist	_____		
Medicine	_____		
Insurance:			
Auto	_____		
Health	_____		
Home/Renters	_____		
Life/Disability	_____		

Exhibit 3–4

Cash Flow Worksheet

Income: Take-home pay _____
Bonuses _____
Self-employment income _____
Rental property income _____
Interest _____
Dividends _____
Other _____
Total income _____

Outgo: Mortgage or rent _____
Property taxes _____
Income tax not withheld _____
Alimony, child support _____
Installment, credit card payments _____
Insurance: Auto _____
Home _____
Life _____
Health, Other _____
Food
Utilities
Transportation (Including Auto) _____
Child care _____
Pocket money _____
Clothing, personal care _____
Medical, dental bills _____
Education expenses _____
Entertainment, gifts, vacations _____
Contributions _____
Miscellaneous _____
Savings _____
Total Outgo _____

Surplus or Deficit (Income minus Outgo) _____

Exhibit 3–5

Annual Expense Worksheet

	Mort. Rent	Prop. Taxes	Income Tax	Credit Cards	Insur.	Food	Util.	Home Impr.	Auto Exp.	Child Care	Clothes	Ent/ Gifts	Cont.	Savings	Misc.	TOTAL
Jan.																
Feb.																
Mar.																
Apr.																
May																
Jun.																
Jul.																
Aug.																
Sep.																
Oct.																
Nov.																
Dec.																
Total																

Services:	Bank 1	Bank 2	Bank 3
Low-fee checking			
Safe Deposit Box			
ATM			
Saturday hours			
Evening hours			
Overdraft protection			

Keep your finances in order. Make a file for your credit card receipts so you can find them quickly to reconcile your bill. If you feel uncomfortable balancing your checking account, either hire someone to do it, or have some friends with the same problem come over for an evening of checkbook balancing. A friend might be able to see the mistake you have consistently missed. You might also turn an unpleasant activity into something fun.

If you are disorganized but have a friend who is an organization whiz, swap talents. Have her organize your file cabinet while you care for her children or give her your time in another way. You may find a commercial calendar-organizer is helpful, or you may want to simply purchase a binder and make charts that work well for you. Experiment until you find a system that fits your lifestyle.

If nothing seems to work and you continue to have no idea where your money is going, consider the possibility that some part of you may not want that information. As long as you do not have the facts, you are not forced to make any changes.

Rule Number 3:   Turn Credit Cards from Foe to Friend

Credit cards can be a good money management tool, or they can be a road to disaster. They offer many advantages, including a built-in

Rosemary has worked as an accountant for 27 years. She has been employed by CPAs most of the time, and has a following of clients who would not consider seeing anyone else. She loves jewelry and always wears just the right pieces to match her outfit.

She said, "I see a lot of clients who are preparing for retirement, yet I don't have much. I've got an IRA, but that's about it. My husband is self-employed, it's a small business and we don't have health insurance, or life insurance, either. He's my second husband, and now, at his age, it's too expensive to buy life insurance.

"One good thing we are doing is taking $300 a month from my salary and adding it to the house payment. That way, the house will be clear in ten years, which will help a lot as a couple, and when one of us dies, the survivor will be in a stable position."

paper trail to track your expenses. Some cards, such as American Express, provide quarterly reports that categorize your spending into defined accounts. When you have credit cards, you can carry less cash, knowing you have the option of getting more through a cash advance, should you need it.

When paid off monthly, credit cards allow you a "float," whereby you make a purchase but do not pay for it until four to six weeks later. If you have the cash to make the purchase but use a credit card instead, this float enables you to earn interest on your money during that time.

Unfortunately, credit cards can cause trouble by providing a relatively easy way to overextend your finances. If you find yourself consistently unable to pay your monthly bills, you might be headed for trouble. Other red flags include:

- being uncertain of the total amount of debt;
- taking out new installment loans before the old ones are paid;
- using a cash advance from one credit card to repay other debts;
- making only the minimum payment on your credit cards;
- consistently owing 20 percent or more of your take-home pay on debts other than your mortgage.

Most people can handle 10 percent debt; many people can manage 15 percent debt, but 20 percent seems to be a breaking point.

To determine the amount of debt you carry, complete the credit summary worksheet shown in Exhibit 3-6. This will force you to look at the big picture and determine the total amount of debt you have.

Take steps to avoid the credit card blues:

- Pay in cash.
- Limit the number of cards you carry.
- Keep track of the amount you owe on the cards you use.
- Throw out credit card applications.
- Tear up and cancel any "extra" cards.

Exhibit 3–6

Your Credit Summary

Name of Creditor	Interest Rate	Monthly Payment	Total Amount Due

Total Monthly
Payment _____

Total
Amount Owed _____

Percent of
Take-Home Pay _____

Strange as it may seem, underspending is also a problem for many women. You might welcome such a problem if you have struggled with excessive debt. Underspending is a trait often found in those who have lived through poverty or who do not trust their own resources to provide a consistent standard of living. The underspender often finds it especially difficult to spend money on herself, although she is often generous when spending for her family and friends.

Ask yourself the following questions to determine if you are an underspender:

- Do you feel a touch of anxiety or guilt whenever you purchase something, even though you can afford it?

- Do friends and family often tell you you should go on vacation and pamper yourself?

- Do you habitually settle for less than you know you can afford and *would enjoy*?

- Do you carry unused travelers' checks for years after you have returned from a trip?

Rule Number 4:   Give Yourself Permission to Spend, Too

Give yourself permission to be more flexible to spend money on yourself by trying these ideas:

- Make a wish list of everything you have always wanted. Certainly, one or two of these items will be within your economic reach now. Purchase one item for yourself today, instead of postponing it indefinitely.

- Observe the financial habits of those around you. Find someone who earns, saves, and spends money in a way you admire. Use that person as a role model for your behavior.

- Give yourself a small present each week, such as a bouquet, a book, or a cassette tape.

- If you truly believe that you cannot afford any unbudgeted extravagance, meet with a professional to discuss ways to increase your disposable income.

Financial savvy begins with being conscious of your current financial position and bringing some insight into why you are where you are. Once a firm foundation is established, change can be made.

Easy Action List

- Prepare a net worth statement and date it.
- Develop a system to track spending patterns.
- Determine if you are an underspender, overspender or appropriate spender. Most of us are all three in certain areas. Look for the overall trend.

Planning Chart—Chapter 3

Your age now:

20s	30s	40s	50s
Examine and record your current financial position	Update and compare progress	Same	Same
Examine spending habits	Evaluate regularly in relation to goals	Same	Same
Establish credit history in your name	Examine credit history annually	Same	Same

Your Health
—Today's Priority, Tomorrow's Promise

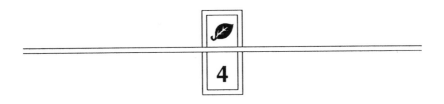

The adage that no one is going to take care of you but you is especially true with respect to healthcare. You must take complete and immediate responsibility for your medical well-being. Everyone ages, yet some seem to show the results less than others. The ideas and suggestions in this chapter are intended as starting points for taking an interest in your health and your physical well-being.

The life span of humans appears to fall between 85 and 115 years. These figures have remained consistent for a long time. Life span is not the same as life expectancy, which is the number of years a person of a specific age or group can expect to continue living. Life span excludes accidents and illness, life expectancy includes them. For example, in 1900 the life expectancy was 47 years. Currently it is 74 and continuing upward because of improved nutrition and the control of disease.[1] The natural life span, however, remains 85 to 115 years.

For each year past age 30, the maximum efficiency of your body decreases approximately 1 to 2 percent. This rate cannot be stopped entirely, although your maximum efficiency can be improved through practice. The earlier you begin, the stronger foundation you will have.

Rule Number 1:   Create an Active Lifestyle; Incorporate an Exercise Program

Physical fitness in general, and mobility in particular, increase with regular exercise. One of the greatest fears people have about old age is the loss of mobility.[2] This dread may be controlled by starting a simple exercise program now and staying with it. Blood pressure, heart capacity, and general reaction time will benefit simultaneously. If you use your body—keeping fit through proper training—you can add extra years to your life.

We do older citizens few favors by expecting them to be less active, by setting them aside from the mainstream of life in retirement communities, and by insisting on retirement at age 65, forcing them into increased financial dependence. Such efforts have served to isolate older people at a time when they need to feel wanted and a vital part of life.

Plan now to include these factors in your goals as you age:

- Be as independent as you can as long as you can—it keeps you alert and active.
- Take control of your habits—the good and the bad.
- Establish a routine of socialization and keep at it. The routine may be modified from time to time, but it should be an important part of your life.
- Keep learning. Something new is always on the next page. School is no longer the arena of the young, as witnessed by the success of Elderhostel (see Chapter 13).

As you increase your years of vigor and activity, it is only logical that you decrease your years of dependence. Many people do not fear death itself, but dread doing a sloppy job of dying. Doing everything you can to remain an active, vital person will reduce that possibility.

Janet's husband had been ill a long time. He had retired before he became ill. She gave up her job as the operations officer of a small regional bank to care for him at home. She has been able to get away from home for short periods of respite, but more and more she has friends from the bank over for lunch. It is the only way she can stay in touch.

She said, "A woman needs a place of her own. Mine is a desk. My husband and I are both at home and it's easy to get in each other's way. I can go to my desk and that's my place and he leaves it alone.

"Also, people should travel while they can. My Bob has a heart condition and we don't go anywhere. He's afraid he won't be able to keep up. He doesn't want me to go anywhere, either, because he might get sick while I'm gone. I'd like to do things, but it's just not possible."

Some rebel against regular exercise because they see themselves changing overnight from a sedentary existence to one involving hours of training each day. But regular exercise means only doing more than you are doing now, and doing it regularly. If you have a lifestyle with limited activity, a simple exercise such as walking for 15 minutes each day could represent a 100 percent increase. If you increase gradually; you'll be more likely to enjoy each dimension along the way.

Easy Action List

- Find an appropriate exercise program for you and your lifestyle.
- Try it for two months, then evaluate your progress.

Rule Number 2: Be Aware of Your Use of Prescription Drugs

Doctors sometimes find it difficult to resist the temptation to over-medicate their elderly patients. Unfortunately, side effects can multiply in your system. Crucial drugs make up less than 10 percent of all prescriptions in the United states. Over 1.5 billion prescriptions are written each year—eight for every person in the country. The proportion is higher for the elderly.[3]

You may need sedatives, tranquilizers, or pain pills for short periods of time in your life, but rid yourself of them as soon as possible. Use prescriptions and medications only when necessary. Ask your physician for alternatives, such as a change in diet or living habits, that would achieve the same results.

Rule Number 3: Speak Up to Your Doctor

Learn to be comfortable asking your doctor questions. It is not rude to take notes while your doctor is giving you information and instructions. You may find it more convenient to take a small, pocket-sized tape recorder and tape the conversation or take a friend along.

After Sally R. discovered a lump in her breast during her regular self-examination, she immediately made an appointment with her doctor.

She thought she was calm and objective about the situation, but the morning before her appointment, she broke a china bowl and was nearly involved in a minor automobile accident. Realizing that she was much more emotionally upset than she had admitted, Sally asked her sister, Carol, to accompany her to the doctor's office. Carol's steady and comforting attitude helped Sally through the tense experience.

When talking to your doctor, it's OK to say:

- Would you go over that point again?
- I don't understand the reason for this prescription.
- What are the risks involved in this procedure?
- Does this drug have any side effects?
- What is the cost?
- Is it necessary for me to go to the hospital for this?
- I want to think about this; I'll let you know tomorrow.
- I'd like another opinion.
- Will this medication have any effect on the other prescriptions that I now take?

Medications are standardized in their preparation at the manufacturing level, and the tasks of local pharmacists include dispensing, record keeping, and relabeling. Comparison shopping by telephone can result in substantial savings to you, but remember convenience is an important factor—location, business hours, and home delivery can make a big difference when you are ill.

Generic drugs are cost-savers. Your telephone survey of pharmacies will help you determine if the generic drug is available. Pharmacies may not stock all generics, but do ask.

Easy Action List

- Examine the contents of your medicine cabinet.
- Discuss with your doctor the medications you no longer need.

Rule Number 4: Review Your Use of Alcohol and Cigarettes

The person who is serious about good health will examine her habits, both good and bad, carefully.

You'll be better off if you don't smoke. Resources are available to help you break the habit once thought glamourous. Hospitals, clinics, health clubs, churches, and consultants all offer "stop smoking" programs. A few minutes on the telephone will bring you enough information to begin a program that fits your schedule and character. For example, the American Lung Association (check your local telephone directory) and the American Cancer Society (1-800-942-6985) present four- and eight-hour programs for a small fee. In addition, a *Five Day Plan to Stop Smoking* series is sponsored by Seventh-Day Adventist Churches. More information may be obtained from the General Conference of Seventh-Day Adventists, Washington, DC 20012, 1-800-253-3000.[4]

Alcohol and chemical substance use should also be carefully reviewed. It is important to balance any social or recreational usage against potential long-term health hazards.

Rule Number 5: What You Eat Makes a Difference

The general trend of public awareness is toward healthier dietary choices. Pay attention to nutrition and good eating habits. Many restaurants feature entrees that are good for you and are identified as such on the menu. You may see the heart symbol printed by an item, a sign that the entree is on the list recommended by the American Heart Association.

Easy Action List

- As you sit down to each meal, survey the food before you. How do you feel about the food you're eating?

- This week, try two new recipes that contribute to a healthier diet.

One of the most common problems found in the older person is a combination of two conditions: diabetes and obesity. Until recently, the practice was to treat all diabetics with medication, but that procedure has been reexamined for individuals with Type II diabetes (called adult onset diabetes, or noninsulin-dependent diabetes mellitus). Type I is juvenile diabetes, which begins in early years and has serious consequences. Type II is a milder form, although neglect may have grave effects. Presently, older overweight diabetics who are able to exercise regularly and lose weight find the symptoms of the disease disappear.[5] Talk to your physician about your risk of diabetes.

The test for diabetes is a simple one, and low-cost clinics often offer it at senior centers and hospital outpatient departments. Watch for the schedule, and include the examination in your regular schedule of health checkups.

Easy Action List

- Make a list of physical conditions you want to be checked for each year.
- Mark your calendar so you remember to have these checkups.

Rule Number 6: Exercise Your Memory as Well as Your Body

Many people appear to become forgetful in old age, but memory can be improved through use, just as the body can become stronger through exercise.

Older people often recall a narrow range of long-past events quite clearly. A valuable activity to help overcome this narrowing is to write your life story. You may have had unpleasant experiences, which have caused you to close off sections of your life, yet when you begin to put your life down on paper, you gain an overall perspective.

Writing about yourself can be an important gift to your family. Many times mothers feel that because they had certain experiences when they were young, their children automatically know and understand those events. The events will be lost if you do not record them. You will also provide valuable information about members of your family and their relationships. Not only can the act of writing serve as a catharsis for you, but it can also offer insight about you to your family.

Easy Action List

- Choose one outstanding event of your childhood.
- Make an outline about that happening, including as much detail as you can recall. As you write, long-forgotten details will appear in your mind's eye.

Rule Number 7:   Try to Delay or Prevent Osteoporosis

Called the "woman's disease," osteoporosis is not a disease, but a preventable condition in which the bones gradually lose calcium, making them weak and brittle.

During your formative years, you stored more calcium in your bones than your body used. It is a natural phenomenon for the body to use body calcium from bone mass. The problem arises when, after menopause, an imbalance occurs due to reduced intake and storage of calcium. Menopause is the turning point, but if a plan of hormone replacement is followed after menopause, the bone mass stays nearly the same as before. Without it, bones can become weaker.

Try to stay active and maintain your calcium intake. When the bone mass stays above a certain threshold, bones are resistant to fractures. When the bone mass drops below the critical level, fractures occur more easily. The trigger in this change is the menopausal loss of the hormone estrogen. You should thoroughly discuss the matter with your physician, since hormone replacement is not advisable for some women.

Calcium is an important element, not only in building bone mass, but in other bodily functions. If you do not ingest enough calcium through diet or by taking supplements, your body will use the calcium stored in your bones. A simple activity, such as walking briskly for 20

Sylvia's convention badge was crowded with symbols of achievement in her service club. She owned a beauty shop, and had hired a competent manager, so she had the time to volunteer for many projects. Sylvia had served on every commit- tee and had been elected to most offices. She could not say no to a nominating committee. She was glad to see Frances again.

Frances was the most senior member of her club, in age and in years of membership. She took great pride in her club and its activities. She and her husband had been in the insurance business together, but she retired after he passed away suddenly. Her life since has been filled with her club. Frances' health has not been good in recent years, but she keeps going one way or another.

Both Frances and Sylvia agreed that retirement brought them no disappointments, "at least not yet."

"The biggest surprise for me," said Sylvia, "is that I am busier than I ever was before. But a woman should have something in mind to do after she retires. I mean something serious, not just a pastime. I am giving a lot of time to tutor-training in a literacy program. I help Spanish-speaking people learn English."

"I agree," said Frances, "Have something in mind, whether you've ever done it before or not. And I would advise women to be sure they can take their health plan with them into retirement. I know that's important with all the trouble I've had with my knees. That insurance means everything."

Sylvia nodded. "Yes, and they should plan ahead financially, and buy the big items, like a car, ahead of retirement when their income is greater."

Frances smiled, "Just tell them it's a wonderful time of life."

minutes or more each day, can make a valuable contribution in maintaining healthy, strong bones. Other factors that contribute to bone loss, and over which you have control, are:

- alcohol
- smoking
- caffeine
- salt
- excess protein

Your increased awareness of nutrition will help you control caffeine, salt, and excess protein. It may also help you avoid the stereotypical injury to an older woman, a broken hip, which involves hospitalization, surgery, and restricted independence for several months. Two other sites in the body are commonly associated with an osteoporosis fracture: the wrist and the spine. Changes in the curvature of the spine are often included as common indications of osteoporosis—older women become stooped and look shrunken.[6]

A similar affliction often related to aging is arthritis. Again, the goal is to slow down the process as much as possible, beginning now. The formula that helps stave off arthritis also strengthens the heart and blood vessels. Keep active through a regular exercise program, one that has enough variety to keep you from being bored. Keep your weight under control, which will reduce unnecessary stress on your joints. Keep your joints protected by being aware of the signals your body sends you.

Rule Number 8: Regular and Thorough Breast Examinations Are a Must

Breast cancer continues to be a major concern for all women. Development of the mammogram has substantially reduced risk from X-ray radiation that many women feared in the past. The procedure is a simple one, and has the advantage of early detection, thus offering a better chance of controlling the disease. Hospitals and clinics often provide examinations and mammograms at certain times of the year at reduced rates. Health insurance may pay all or part of the cost. Phone for information and include this important step in your regular health routine.

Regular breast self-examination is an essential part of your health maintenance program. The correct techniques are spelled out clearly in a brochure supplied by the American Cancer Society. Phone your local chapter for a copy of it.

Good health management is as important as the management of your investment portfolio. Consider the time and effort you spend in this arena as an investment in your future. The degree to which you will be able to enjoy life may depend upon self-discipline in taking care of your health.

Rule Number 9: Keep Your Self-Respect Level High

Your psychological health is as important as your physical health. The way you feel about yourself is reflected in almost every aspect of your life. Messages bombard you from every direction on the importance of being young or youthful looking—messages usually relating to purchasing a certain product. Many people who are not young or beautiful are attractive and fascinating companions because they begin with solid self-esteem.

Self-esteem is a much-used phrase, but the basic concept of respect for one's inner self is valid. The question of "Who am I?" that we faced early in life occurs again in our evaluation of ourselves and our accomplishments as we age.

Perception is reality. If you perceive that you are ugly, clumsy, or inept, you are likely to live down to that image. On the other hand, if you are confident and realistic in your talents and skills, your abilities will be recognized and respected by others.

Sometimes it takes the vision of others to observe ability and talent. Take the case of James Sweeney, a teacher at Tulane University. Intensely interested in computers and convinced he could teach anyone to be computer-literate, he selected a person who had been identified as one who was unsuited for, and would never master, computer technology. By using advanced teaching techniques centering on self-esteem and high expectations, the subject not only became computer-literate, but found a new career as manager of a computer operation, with responsibilities that included programming and training of staff. Congratulations to them both![7]

Easy Action List

- Identify one skill you have that you would like to improve, or one that you would like to have.

- Take the first step in becoming proficient in that activity. Then take the next step.

Rule Number 10: Plan for the Health Needs of Parents and Parents-in-Law

Marilyn K. was the advertising director for a department store in the Northwest, when she took an emergency leave from her position to return to her former home in the Midwest. The reason: To take charge of placing her elderly father in a nursing home. Her mother, who had taken care of her husband as best as she could for many months, could no longer manage. She was unable to make the many decisions that were necessary. Marilyn spent several grueling weeks making arrangements. Finally, exhausted, she said to the nursing home manager, "I've got to get my brothers involved in this problem. I can't go on like this forever." The answer from the manager: "Don't count on it." The manager had seen too many cases where the woman in the family was expected to do everything.

Caring for elderly parents or parents-in-law is a task that often falls on women. You will be better prepared if you can:

- discuss their wishes with them long before the need. "Mom, I'm making out my will. Do you and Dad have one?"

- determine who will share the tasks and costs with you. Siblings who live nearest may bear a disproportionate share of both.

- divide your responsibility between your parents and your family at home. Have other family members help.

Discussion of these items may take place over a considerable period of time, and adjustments may be made as conditions change. Start the conversation now.

Easy Action List

- Introduce the subject to your parents, giving them the greatest opportunity to choose.
- Listen with understanding and care to their fears and concerns. Help them list their goals.
- Ask your spouse and children for their input.

The role of care-giver also may include a wife caring for a disabled husband. The tasks can be overwhelming, both physically and emotionally. Numerous opportunities for support are available from home health care services, day care programs, and other related public and private services. Reaching out for assistance helps the care-giver provide better quality attention, and preserves her strength, as well. Family members, including older children, should accept responsibility. Clear instructions and understanding of each role will bring the family closer together, and this will be especially comforting to the disabled person.

Do not try to carry the entire burden yourself. By doing so, you will shut out others who could benefit from the experience. Your telephone directory is a good starting place to find occasional or regular help. Check under your county health department; private care providers also are available. Your local hospital, family doctor, or nurse may give you leads and recommendations. In this situation, you must preserve your health to give better care to another.

One of the joys of middle-life is confidence in yourself, gained by years of experience at the art of living. If you have planned and managed those elements that might be barriers, especially those related to health and care-giving, you will have the inner satisfaction that you have done the best you could with what you were given to work with.

Endnotes

1. Fries, James F., M.D., and Vickery, Donald M., M.D., *Take Care of Yourself: The Consumer's Guide to Medical Care* (Reading, Mass.: Addison-Wesley Publishing Company, 1987), p. 36.

2. Ibid. , p. 37.

3. Ibid., p. 45.

4. "A Quitter's Profile." *University of California, Berkeley, Wellness Letter* (July 1990), no. 10, p. 7.

5. Fries and Vickery, op. cit., p. 46.

6. *Every Woman's Guide to Osteoporosis: How to Prevent It, How to Live with It.* (Daly City, Calif.: Krames Communications, 1986), pp. 4-13.

7. Rosenthal, Robert, and Jacobson, Lenore. *Pygmalion in the Classroom* (New York: Holt, Rinehart and Winston, Inc., 1986), p. 3.

Planning Chart—Chapter 4

Your age now:

20s	30s	40s	50s
Begin regular exercise program	Continue program	Same	Same
Study nutrition and practice good eating habits	Same	Same	Same, modify as necessary
Quit smoking	Same	Same	Same
		Begin to write the story of your family	Continue project
	Consult your parents about their wishes for healthcare later	Same, plus discusssion with your siblings and your children	Same, refine details and be ready to put plans into action

Your Insurance Options

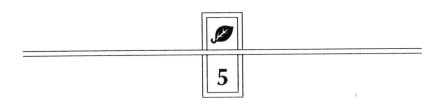

5

Insurance is protection from risks that you cannot afford to cover. While no one disputes the importance of insurance, many people feel overwhelmed with the costs and options involved, or are put off by the confusing terms and language common to the industry.

First, determine whether you actually need life insurance. Most people never entertain this fundamental question. Life insurance is necessary only if someone else is dependent upon your income. The amount of life insurance you buy should be calculated to suit your individual needs.

Marge C. is divorced and has no children. Since no one is dependent upon her income and she has enough assets to cover any final expenses, she does not carry life insurance. Marge, however, is concerned about her parents' well being. Her parents are living on Social Security and her father's pension, but if Marge's father dies first, Marge would have to contribute to her mother's support. If Marge's assets are not substantial, Marge should purchase some life insurance on her own life at that time. It might be argued that Marge should purchase life insurance sooner when it is less expensive. But by waiting, Marge will have use of that money for investments, and the circumstances may never dictate that she needs life insurance.

Rule Number 1:   Buy Only the Life Insurance You Need

Numerous ways exist to determine the right amount of life insurance coverage. Some experts suggest you add a zero to the wage-earner's income. So, if you earned $40,000 a year, you would need $400,000 worth of life insurance. Others suggest more complex formulas.

Take a common-sense approach. Think about a period of time, two years, for example, during which you would not have to make any lifestyle changes. That is, you would not have to worry about getting a job or changing the job you have, or moving, or selling anything you did not want to sell. Estimate expenses during that time frame. Now estimate the amount of years you would expect the need to continue. That is, how long this money will be needed (for example, for your spouse's expected life). Add to that amount any major expenses, such as college tuition. Add a buffer to offset inflation. Subtract annual income from other investments and other assets, again multiplying by the number of years you expect the need to continue. That amount (which may well seem astoundingly large) would be one recommended amount. If you want a more detailed calculation, complete Worksheet 1.

Easy Action List

- Calculate the recommended amount for you.
- Check the answer against your present insurance coverage.

Two basic types of insurance are available—with or without a savings plan. Term life insurance is pure protection and works in a manner similar to car insurance. It is in force for a specific period, or term. If death does not occur during that time period, you start all over with a new time frame and a new cost. As you grow older, the insurance premium rises. No savings provisions are included in term plans.

Worksheet 1

Deciding How Much Life Insurance You Need

Needs	Amount

Immediate Expenses

1. Funeral costs _____

2. Uninsured medical costs _____

Long-Term Needs

1. Emergency fund _____

2. Repayment of debts _____

3. Family income _____

4. Education fund _____

5. Retirement fund _____

6. Homemaking expenses _____

Total Needs _____

Assets

1. Current life insurance _____

2. Any pension benefits _____

3. Cash and savings _____

4. Equity in real estate (if it is to be sold) _____

5. Investments (stocks, bonds, mutual
    funds, IRAs, and Keogh plans) _____

Total Assets _____

Insurance Calculation

Total Needs _____

less

Total Assets _____

Life Insurance Needed _____

Life insurance policies that include some kind of savings program are whole life, endowment, and universal. With this type of insurance you pay a set annual premium that does not rise as you grow older, and you may borrow from the cash value. The amount of life insurance benefit paid is reduced by the amount of the outstanding loan.

Controversy surrounds the appropriateness of term over other types of insurance. Each proponent presents a strong case. Remember that your agent will receive a percentage of the first-year premium.

Rule Number 2:   Evaluate the Need for Life Insurance on a Regular Basis

This rule is especially appropriate when you have a lifestyle change. Dick and Judy R. got married and, like many newlyweds, purchased insurance for Dick. On the advice of their insurance agent, they purchased a $150,000 whole life policy. Since the insurance payment was automatically taken out of Dick's checking account, they never reevaluated the decision until Judy began getting interested in the family finances and asked Dick about the policy. Many changes had occurred during the 10 years Dick and Judy had been married. Judy had changed careers and was now making more money than her husband. The house payment could easily be made from either paycheck. They had no children or outstanding debts. They decided they no longer needed life insurance on Dick, surrendered the policy, and invested the cash value that had accumulated in the policy. The money they formerly spent for premium payments was put into a mutual fund.

Easy Action List

- Gather together all your life insurance policies.
- Evaluate your position.

The need for disability insurance is greater than for life insurance because the likelihood of becoming disabled is higher than the likelihood of death for younger adults. Since disability insurance under Social Security has severe limitations, check your benefit package at work (and your spouse's if you are married) and examine the disability coverage. If you are not covered, explore purchasing a private policy. Remember, Social Security pays benefits only when a disability is expected to last a year or more, or is likely to result in death.

Rule Number 3:   Give Disability Insurance a High Priority

Disability insurance provides an income should you become sick or injured and unable to work. It protects against family financial catastrophe by giving income to meet your daily expenses. You receive a flat amount in lieu of salary, but it does not pay medical or hospital expenses. Shop for the best coverage available. Use these points to compare policies:

- Choose a disability policy that is guaranteed renewable and cannot be canceled.

- Find "own occupation" coverage for professional and white-collar workers that will pay as long as you are unable to do your regular job. For example, a surgeon might fall and break her wrist, making it impossible to perform surgery, although she could still practice medicine through consultations and teaching. With this clause she would receive disability coverage because she could not perform her primary occupation.

- Choose a policy with "proportionate" or "residual" benefits. If you lost half your normal income, you would get 50 percent of the policy's monthly payouts.

- Make sure the elimination period—the time between the disability and first payment—suits your situation. The longer the period, the lower the premium, but you must have savings that will cover expenses for that period.

Easy Action List

- Review your disability coverage.
- Shop for private policy if needed.

The cost of medical insurance continues to rise with terrifying speed. If you are not covered by a plan, you must purchase a private plan. The risk is too high to be uncovered. One way to keep costs lower is to have a higher deductible amount and be willing to use predesignated doctors and hospitals. With a high deductible, be sure to save that amount for possible use. When you require medical treatment, shop the cost of services if time allows.

Maggie B. was told she needed to have a breast biopsy. Her medical insurance deductible amount was $2,000, so Maggie would be responsible for the cost. She could have the biopsy performed as an out-patient in one of three locations in her town. After calling each facility, she found a difference of $600 in the cost of the operating room. Maggie was able to save $600 by making three phone calls and using the least-expensive but completely adequate facility. She learned that by paying for the room one day in advance, she was able to save another 10 percent. After this experience, she called the various labs in town to compare the cost of preoperation lab work. She was again able to save by planning in advance.

Rule Number 4:   Save Money by Comparing Costs

Most people do not shop prices for medical facilities. Even if you have no deductible to worry about, you may be required to make a co-payment. Spend time comparing prices to save money. You may encounter some resistance or surprise from your doctor. Remember, there's no reason to be embarrassed about examining both the financial and the medical arrangements.

Insurance for long-term nursing home care should also be considered. For many people, protection against that possibility is worth the price. Some insurance companies are responding to this need for healthcare through special riders on universal life insurance policies. These policies generally allow the owner to use the death benefit when confined to a nursing facility. The conditions vary significantly, so understand the policy thoroughly. Variations may include:

- the maximum amount payable each month
- length of time payments will be made
- whether or not a hospital stay is required before nursing home costs will be paid

Rates and policies differ tremendously. A clear picture of the kind of coverage you want and can afford will protect you from sales pitches.

When you shop for insurance, it is important to find an agent who will present facts accurately and service your account appropriately. An insurance agent is paid a high percentage of the first year's premium and a much smaller percentage after that, so be aware of the salesperson's compensation and bias while listening to the initial presentation. Enter the discussion with a good idea of what you need and want. Be cautious about signing any paperwork at the time of the first meeting. Discuss your situation with at least two agents before making a final decision.

The agent also gets paid from every premium payment you make, so insist on proper service. Second and subsequent year commissions are lower than the initial commission, so the agent doesn't have as much incentive to continue to treat you well. If you do not receive appropriate service, transfer your account to another agent or another company.

Easy Action List

- Keep a list of contacts (meetings, correspondence, etc.) with your agent in your notebook.
- Evaluate the service.

In addition to adequate insurance coverage, it is essential to have cash set aside for emergencies. Emergency expenses are unanticipated crises, not property taxes or car insurance that is due annually.

The standard guideline is to have three to six months of living expenses available. That standard can be revised under certain conditions. Consider such variables as the amount of time you have been employed with your organization and the likelihood of being dismissed. If you are a teacher with tenure, for example, your greatest need may be to have an adequate disability insurance policy instead of a large emergency fund.

By contrast, if you are self-employed or are new on a job, it is wise to keep a larger emergency fund. Consider your ability to get a signature loan or a cash advance on your credit card. The easier it is to get money quickly from another source, the less cash you have to keep readily available. Be sure you have the ability to repay the loan quickly without accruing large finance charges or overextending yourself.

Easy Action List

- Calculate six months' income.
- Note cash sources to cover this amount.

It is essential to purchase insurance to cover the possibility of loss. The proper amount of insurance also will provide a peace of mind that allows freedom to pursue other interests.

Planning Chart—Chapter 5

Your age now:

20s	30s	40s	50s
Read and understand health insurance policy	Same	Same	Same
	Examine need for adequate life insurance	Evaluate need	Same
	Examine need for adequate disability insurance	Evaluate need	Same

Your Pension Plan
—What Does It Mean to You?

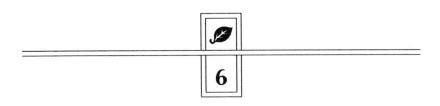

6

One of the major points you learn as you prepare for retirement is that Social Security is not enough—it was never meant to be. Every woman, whether self-employed, employed by a major corporation, or any size company in between, must protect herself financially.

All women who earn income that is reported to the Internal Revenue Service are eligible to contribute to Individual Retirement Accounts (IRAs). The maximum amount a woman can invest each year is either $2,000 or the total amount earned, if less than $2,000. Because many women work for smaller companies that do not provide company pension plans, it is essential that women take advantage of IRAs. Individual Retirement Accounts became very popular when the amount contributed could be deducted from your income tax. Laws have changed, however, so that now the amount deducted, if any, is dependent upon your total income and the availability of a company pension plan. Because of these restrictions, many investors have lost their enthusiasm for IRAs. The major advantage of the IRA is not the deductibility of the contribution but that the contribution compounds tax-deferred until withdrawal (see Exhibit 6-1).

Once you contribute to an IRA you cannot use the money before age 59-1/2 without a 10 percent penalty paid to the IRS. In addition to the penalty, the money withdrawn will be taxed as income for the year. If the investor waits until she is 59-1/2 to withdraw the money, she pays tax only on the amount withdrawn. You must begin withdrawing money by the time you are 70-1/2.

There is a wide range of choices for your IRA investment, including stocks, bonds, mutual funds, and certificates of deposit. There are some restrictions, however. You cannot, for example, invest in gold or silver coins or use your IRA to help purchase your primary residence. The type of investment you choose will depend upon the amount of risk you want to take. Some people believe that you cannot lose money in an IRA. Unfortunately, you can lose money, and the loss is not deductible on your income tax.

The self-employed woman will need to set up her own pension plan. Two plans are available for small business owners and their employees: the Keogh and the Simplified Employee Pension Plan (SEP). The SEP is the easier to set up and requires less paperwork for the Internal Revenue Service (IRS).

The rules for both plans are similar to the regulations governing Individual Retirement Accounts (IRAs). The major difference is that each of these plans allows a higher limit than the $2,000 ceiling for an IRA. The amount invested is a percentage of the net profit of your business. Work closely with your accountant to follow the correct procedure.

Beyond the IRA, an employed woman should first look to her employer for a pension plan. Keep pensions in mind when changing jobs, or when discussing benefits with your employer. A retirement plan should be an important element in agreeing on the conditions of your employment. Employers are not obligated under the law to provide pension plans for their employees, but most large companies and public agencies offer a plan of some type, and some offer more than one.

Exhibit 6-1

An Individual Retirement Account Illustration

$2,000 Per Year—Accumulating Tax-Deferred at 10% Per Year

If You Are This Old	You Have These Years to Age 65	With an IRA Plan, Your Total Investment Will Be:	The Value of Your IRA Plan at Age 65 Will Be:	The Value of Your Account Without an IRA, Assuming 30% Tax Bracket*:
30	35	$70,000	$610,508	$204,408
33	32	64,000	447,366	162,036
35	30	60,000	362,835	138,347
38	27	54,000	263,877	108,487
40	25	50,000	212,603	91,793
43	22	44,000	152,578	70,750
45	20	40,000	121,477	58,986
48	17	34,000	85,067	44,156
50	15	30,000	66,202	35,866
53	12	24,000	44,117	25,416
55	10	20,000	32,674	19,573
58	7	14,000	19,277	12,209
60	5	10,000	12,366	8,091

*These results reflect $1,400 invested annually ($2,000 minus 30% in taxes), growing at 7% annually (10% minus 30% in taxes).

After you have verified that your company has a plan, make sure you are eligible to participate. Many women work part-time or seasonally and do not meet the minimum qualifications of their employer's plan. Even if they qualify and contribute, women who move often with their families may withdraw their contributions to help finance a new house or pay moving costs. This seems especially likely to happen in military families. Consider Ann D., the wife of a Navy Chief Petty Officer, who moved often during the 17 years of her marriage. She was a kindergarten teacher and worked in the public schools wherever her husband was stationed. Each time they moved, she withdrew her pension funds to cover extra expenses. When they were divorced, not only was she without any pension reserve but he had cleaned out their bank accounts, and she had very little with which to start a new life. His pension, of course, remained intact.

If you are eligible under your husband's pension, verify how you are covered and exactly what your coverage would be in case you are widowed. Statistics show that most wives outlive their husbands, so this is a critical factor. The materials given to him at the time of enrollment may cover this point. If not, write the plan administrator for details.

Employers often offer some type of savings plan that allows employees to put away pretax dollars until retirement. These are often referred to as 401(k) plans (from the IRS authorization section), or deferred compensation, or perhaps a tax-sheltered annuity. A voluntary and specified amount is deducted from your gross pay and invested, then income taxes are calculated on the balance of the money you have earned.

Keep in mind that when you withdraw it after age 59-1/2, you will have to pay income taxes on this money and the interest it has earned. (If you withdraw these funds before the age of 59-1/2, a penalty is assessed in addition to the tax liability.)

The argument for this type of savings is usually made that your taxes will be lower when you retire, meaning that your retirement income will probably be less and, therefore, your tax liability will be less. This

Carmen did not resemble her namesake at all. She was blonde and fair, a Nordic image. When people commented on the discrepancy, as they often did, she explained that her father had been fond of opera. Her sister's name was Mimi.

Carmen was recently widowed, and, because her husband had always taken care of their financial matters, she hardly knew where to begin. Jim had been a high school biology teacher. He had died of a heart attack on his way home from school one Wednesday. Carmen knew he was covered by the teachers' retirement plan in the state where they lived. She went to the headquarters of the school district to inquire about his pension and the benefits that would cover her and their eleven-year-old daughter.

The district payroll clerk waited on Carmen, and was forced to deliver bad news. Jim had never changed the beneficiary on his retirement plan from his ex-wife to Carmen, even though he and Carmen had been married fifteen years, and his ex-wife had moved to another city. Under the laws of the state and his retirement system, Carmen and her daughter got nothing, neither the death benefit nor the return of his contributions. Jim's ex-wife got it all.

is not always the case. Tax laws change, and taxes may be more than you anticipate. The best protection for this type of savings is to diversify. The company offering these plans usually provides several options for placement of funds, such as a mutual fund of equity stocks, a bond fund, a guaranteed income fund, and, of course, the company's own stock.

Employees have a tendency to buy stock in the company where they work. Management encourages the idea because it ensures staff loyalty, and incentives may be offered to stimulate such purchases, *but* employees may lose both their savings and their jobs, depending on the fate of the company. Diversify your company stock by establishing a percentage of your holdings to keep and a percentage to sell. Replace the sold portion with another investment. You may consider another issue in the same industry or balance it with bonds (debt money balanced with equity money). Purchasing company stock in an incentive plan is a good way to save, if you diversify to protect your savings from unforeseen catastrophes.

The two categories of pension plans most often offered by companies are Defined Benefit Plans and Defined Contribution Plans. They have important distinctions.

Defined Benefit Plans provide a specific monthly payment when you retire; that is, you will know exactly what you will receive on a regular basis and can plan your lifestyle accordingly. Sometimes, instead of stating a flat dollar amount that will be given to a person who retires under the plan, a formula is applied to standard factors, such as the number of years of service multiplied by salary at retirement. A percentage of your regular paycheck is paid into the plan by you or by your employer, or both.[1]

Defined Contribution Plans depend on specific amounts being deposited into the plan, either by percentage of salary or stated dollar amounts by you and/or your employer, *but* no benefit amount is known before retirement, since contributions and returns on investments are not yet known. This type of plan usually, but not always, pays a lump-sum amount at the time of retirement. Some of these plans are called 401(k) savings, money purchase, deferred profit, or target benefits.[2] The amount of the benefit will, of course, depend directly on the skill and expertise of the fund manager, whose job it is to invest, protect, and enhance the principal.

Be aware of certain conditions. Suppose a couple works for different companies and both earn the same salary. If she pays into a pension plan and he does not (because his employer pays the full contribution), he earns more when you compare net salaries. This would, of course, be the same if her employer made the entire contribution, and his did not. The point is the employer-only contribution plan allows a greater take-home pay, yet provides retirement benefits.

The two types of plans have another very important difference. Only the Defined Benefit Plan is eligible for coverage by the Pension Benefit Guaranty Corporation (PBGC), one of three agencies of the United States government charged with protecting workers' retirement plans. The Corporation insures over 110,000 private sector plans, covering about 40 million workers.[3] The other two agencies are the Internal Revenue Service, which watches plan funding and other requirements, and the Department of Labor, which oversees fund managements as specified in the Employee Retirement Income Security Act of 1974 (ERISA).[4]

ERISA established protection for workers through minimum provisions for insurance coverage, funding, reporting, and disclosure. Not all plans are covered under this Act. Some exceptions include government, certain church, and fraternal plans, or savings programs that do not provide retirement benefits. Even if your plan is not covered by ERISA, the following elements are basic to your understanding of pension plans generally.

Someone is in charge of every plan, and that person is usually called the *plan administrator*. Under the law, this person is obligated to provide certain information to you, the worker. This information includes a:

- *Summary Plan Description*, which describes how the plan operates, when you are eligible for your benefits, how to calculate your benefit amount, and how to file a claim. You must receive this information within 90 days of participating in the plan. All changes in the plan must be sent to you.

- *Summary Annual Report*, which shows the financial transactions of your plan, and must be given to you annually. The Summary Annual Report may be confusing to interpret or understand. The Pension Rights Center, a nonprofit organization that focuses on pension issues, has produced a helpful booklet, "Protecting Your Pension Money." You may order directly from the Center: Suite 704, 918 16th St., N.W., Washington, DC 20006. The cost is $6.

- *Survivor Coverage Data*, which describes coverage for your spouse or for you, if you are a beneficiary on your husband's plan.

These three items may be requested in writing from your plan administrator, who should be able to answer your questions and clarify matters for you. If you obtain your Summary Annual Report and you do not understand it, ask for an explanation from the plan administrator, your personnel or payroll department, or a union representative.

Easy Action List

- Start a file for all your pension plan information. Keep all your statements together.
- Keep your paycheck stubs.

Another helpful report to have is the Individual Benefit Statement, which shows the dollar amounts you have earned and deposited in the plan, and whether you have a permanent right to receive benefits.[5] Some plans issue this statement on a regular basis, others do not. If yours does not, you may obtain one by requesting it in writing. The plan administrator is obligated to provide one for you, although not more frequently than once a year.[6] If you receive your statement but do not understand it or know how to interpret it, don't be too self-conscious to ask. You have a legitimate right to know. Keep these documents in your permanent records; perhaps in your notebook or file. After you have earned the right to a pension (which is called *being vested*), benefits data must be given to you. Do not overlook this important detail; it may make a difference to you later.

If you have problems obtaining the information described above, you may ask for assistance from the Division of Technical Assistance and Inquiries, Pension and Welfare Benefits Administration, Department of Labor, 200 Constitution Ave., N.W., Washington, DC 20210. This agency was specifically formed to resolve differences and answer questions for plan members.

Rule Number 1: Obtain the Basic Information About Your and/or Your Spouse's Pension Plan on a Regular Basis

Study the material and ask questions if you do not understand it. Union representatives are often well versed in the details of the plan, and staff in the personnel department of your company may serve as a resource as well. The Pension Rights Center, at the address given earlier, publishes a booklet, "Directory of Pension Assistance Resources." The cost is $3.

General Provisions and Terms

In most cases, you, the worker, must meet minimum age and service requirements to participate in a plan, and you cannot be excluded as too old, even if you are hired near the retirement age named in the plan. Generally, a worker must have one year of service and be at least 21 years of age to participate. Two years of service may be mandatory, provided that the plan gives full and immediate vesting.

Find out how the plan defines a year of service. Often, it means a 12-month period when you were in paid status for at least 1,000 hours, including sick leave and vacation time. It may also include any back-pay awards you have received.

Shirley L. went to work part-time for an electronics firm when her daughter started school. She worked three hours a day for two years, then quit to take care of her husband's elderly parents. After they passed away, she returned to the plant in another department, this time working five hours a day. She was not given credit in the retirement plan for her first job because she had not worked the minimum number of hours to qualify. Employers sometimes create part-time jobs so that employees in these jobs will not qualify for retirement plans or other benefits. They do this as a cost-saving measure.

Connie R., a teacher, worked after the birth of her baby, but then decided that she was really needed at home. She quit during spring break because it seemed a logical time to leave. What she did not know was if she had worked just five and a half days more, she would have received a full year's service credit. As it was, she got no credit at all. She did not know the rules, and did not think to ask. The best method of self-protection is to inquire about the pension rules before making job-related decisions. Connie might have saved her credit if she had taken a leave of absence for a specific period, rather than quitting outright.

The best course is to *ask* and make notes. Details that may be important to you later may not seem significant at the time of your conversation with the plan administrator. Unfamiliar items or terms can be confusing. Your notes will help you understand the benefits of the plan.

Plans under ERISA are permitted to use the "elapsed time" method, an alternate way of calculating service. The total period of time worked from the date of employment is used, instead of counting actual hours worked.[7]

When you have met the minimum service requirement, you become vested. This means you have a legal right to receive some or all of your plan benefits at retirement. To collect benefits, you need not be working for the same company when you retire. When you are vested, your right to that benefit, or portion of benefit, remains unchanged, even though you change employers. If you change employers *before*

you are vested, you may lose some or all of your benefits, although you always have the right to recover the contributions you made, plus interest.

Rule Number 2:   Find Out When You Became or Will Become Vested in Your Plan

Vesting must be provided in a minimum time-frame by one of the two following methods:

1. *Cliff vesting* occurs in a single-employer plan; the workers must be vested after no more than five years of service. The worker has no right to retirement benefits until this service requirement has been fulfilled. If she leaves the company before that time, she is only entitled to the return of her contributions plus interest.

2. *Graded vesting* occurs on a graduated schedule, where the worker is at least 20 percent vested after three years' service, and receives 20 percent more for each of the next four years, causing her to be fully vested no later than the completion of seven years' service.

A *break in service*, defined as a year in which a worker did not complete more than 500 hours in paid status, can reduce your vesting ability or your benefits. You need to know the effect of a "break in service." If you worked full-time for three years, then changed to a part-time job of less than 10 hours per week, you might have a break in service and be required to start all over again to become vested when you return to full-time work. *But* if you take a pregnancy or adoption leave, up to 501 hours will be counted as service and will not be considered as a break. Military service in times of war or national emergency is not counted as a break in service. Because of the break-in-service rules, be sure you are aware of the conditions of your plan before you make job-change decisions, especially about moving into a part-time job.[8]

Social Security and Your Pension
Some pension plans are affected by Social Security benefits, in a process called integrating. This means your pension benefit may be

reduced if you are also drawing Social Security. Due to a change in the law, your benefit payment cannot be reduced by more than half because of integration with Social Security; however, this applies only to years worked after 1988. If your plan adjusts for Social Security before that date, your pension may be affected. Some government pensions have the same effect on Social Security. If a Social Security retirement benefit is drawn as a widow, the benefit may be integrated, but no reduction takes place if the widow draws Social Security under her own account.

Jane D. is a widow, and is entitled to a widow's pension under Social Security. Her husband always paid the maximum tax and his Social Security benefit was at the high end of the scale. Jane worked for several years at a city library—enough to be vested in its pension plan. She had a clerical job with low pay. Her own Social Security account reflected her lower salary. At retirement, she discovered that if she drew her library pension, her Social Security widow's pension would be reduced $1 for every $2 of her library pension. She was better off, but only slightly so, to take the library benefit and her Social Security benefit from her own account. Social Security rules penalize the person who has a pension from a tax-supported agency through the use of this reduction. It is called the "double dipping" rule and was designed to prevent well-paid people from collecting two pensions from public funds. It was written for a few but it affects many.

Rule Number 3:   Consult with Social Security and Your Own Pension Plan Advisers Before Making Retirement Choices

Other Options
When you are making retirement plans, you and your income may be affected by decisions relating to:

- early retirement. Some plans allow early retirement, but have an optimal time to retire. Find out when that is.

- survivor's benefits. Many plans allow the worker to take a reduced retirement allowance, and her spouse would continue to receive a percentage of her pension after her death. She may specifically decline the survivor's benefit, but it must be done in writing. Careful attention should be given to this option. Most women outlive their husbands—if he dies first, her pension, at a reduced level because of this choice, may be inadequate for her needs. When this option is chosen, it can *never* be changed.

Survivor's benefits cover the worker before and after her retirement. Payment of a monthly amount may be delayed under the terms of the plan, however, until the normal retirement age. This is similar to Social Security, where the widow's pension is not available until age 60 (then at a reduced amount).

A woman may have to wait until a specified date to draw a pension from her husband's plan if:

- she has been a homemaker and has no plan of her own.
- she has only worked part-time outside the home and does not qualify for a plan of her own.
- she is not old enough to collect under her husband's plan upon his death.

The survivor's benefits, after the worker has retired, must be at least 50 percent of the retiree's benefit, and that amount continues for the rest of the survivor's life. Since the period of payment covers two people, instead of one, the monthly retirement payment to the worker may be considerably lower under the survivor's benefit option. Calculate the benefit both ways before you make a final choice.

Caution: For some workers who terminated employment before 1985 (1987 for some union-negotiated plans), the spouse may not receive a survivor's benefit. Check this with your plan administrator. [9]

The insurance agent may offer you the election of the no-survivor clause, to be supplemented with the purchase of a life insurance policy. In this case, the scenario would read:

- Husband has pension, and retires.

The first thing people noticed about Lorena was her smile. It lit her entire face.

Gladys, standing opposite her, had worked for only two employers in her career. She spent the last 20 years in the billing office of a large utility company. She had worked her way up to section supervisor when she suddenly decided to retire. It took Lorena longer to make the change.

The two women were standing near the punch bowl at a reception for members of a women's club. Lorena leaned forward to make a point. "I'm so glad I retired early. This is the life."

Gladys nodded in agreement.

"But I prepared carefully," Lorena went on. "When I first went to work for the bank, years ago, all they talked about was loyalty, loyalty, loyalty. Well, I learned over time that they weren't going to be loyal to me if it suited them to do something else. I saw what they did to others. I figured I had better have a plan of my own."

She explained that she worked in the escrow department and was good at it. She became active in a professional organization for escrow officers, was president of her local chapter and held a chairmanship in the state organization. When talking to a client one day, the dean of the local community college, she mentioned that there was no place members of her organization could go to get formal training in procedures essential in escrow work. The next thing she knew, she was teaching an evening class.

"I loved the teaching part, and I loved working at the bank, but I could see that this could not go on forever. I had to have a backup plan. I took my knowledge of escrow and built on it. I went back to school and got my real estate broker's license."

The bank's administration did not approve of her having her license, considering it a conflict of interest. At the time she was not working in real estate, just holding the license. The officials wanted her to give it up. She offered to put it on inactive status, but that was not satisfactory to them.

"I decided I had to do what was best for me for a change. I was vested in our retirement plan and I had saved. What a life I have now!"

Gladys nodded with a smile. "I know what you mean. I worked for 25 years, and one day, I just decided that this was it. My job was stressful and I just didn't need all that guff any more. My husband still works, but with my company pension, his when he retires, and the investments we've made, we'll be OK. I wanted to have something to do, so I sell Avon products to a set of regular customers. I take classes for fun and have a great time. Other women can do that, too, if they start early. But you have to have a really sound financial base."

Lorena agreed, then fished in her purse a moment and said, "Do you have my card?"

- Husband chooses option that gives greatest monthly payments, one without any survivor's payment from the pension plan directly.

- Husband buys life insurance policy on his life, with the wife as beneficiary; when he dies she gets a benefit, and in the meantime, they have a larger income.

Sound good? Only if the *wife* is the owner of the life insurance policy. If the original scenario is in place, but the couple is divorced, he owns the life insurance policy and can name anyone he chooses as beneficiary; she has nothing.

Divorce or separation may have a profound effect on pension rights and distribution. Consult your attorney and show her or him your pension's Summary Plan Description and other related information. This is a strong negotiating point; keep in mind that pension benefits may be worth more than a house. Present-day settlements should be calculated to include inflationary changes for years to come.

Rule Number 4: Before You Retire, Understand All of the Options Your Plan Offers

The options can generally be divided into two major categories: annuities and lump-sum payouts. If you have a life-only annuity, it means you have an irreversible contract with the company to pay you a specific amount of money until you die. With this choice you will never outlive your money. Several distribution variations exist. You may choose to have the money paid out in equal amounts as long as you and your spouse live, or you can choose to have a lesser amount paid to a surviving spouse. The danger with the annuity choice is that the dollar amount is never adjusted upward to reflect inflation.

A lump-sum payment, rather than regular and equal checks, may be an option under your plan. That means you have the choice of rolling over the total amount of money into a self-directed IRA. The advantage of this option is that you are in charge both of investment choices and of when withdrawals are made. In other words, if your lump sum amounted to $100,000, you could roll over that amount and invest it in a combination of stocks, mutual funds, bonds, and certificates of deposit. Depending on your management skill and expertise, you could maximize your investment and end up with more income than the other options provided in your plan. As with the other options, you will be taxed on the amount you withdraw.

The danger with this second method is that no guarantees exist. The investments operate as they would outside an IRA. If you make poor choices, the investments will decrease in value, and you will suffer the subsequent reduction in income.

The lump-sum option can also provide another variation. You can take the money, pay tax on it according to a preferred tax rate, and then invest the money any way you wish with no restrictions. Again, there are no guarantees. You have the chance of acquiring far more than you would if you chose an annuity option, but the threat of loss exists as well.

Rule Number 5:   Use Your Calculator and Project All the Options Before You Make Final Changes

If Things Go Wrong

If you should have your claim denied, or if the amount is in dispute, you must be notified in writing by the plan administrator, including specific details of the plan that apply in your case. You have the right to appeal if you do not agree with the decision of the plan administrator. The procedure for this is spelled out in the Summary Plan Description. You are protected from being discharged, fined, or discriminated against if you exercise your rights under ERISA. Such action would bring stiff penalties, including imprisonment.[10]

As mentioned earlier, pension plans vary in their sources of funding. Yours may be funded through contributions from you and your employer, your employer alone, or more than one employer. In Defined Benefit Plans, employers must pay enough each year to cover the cost of the plan, that is, cover the amount the participants earned that year. Or they must get a waiver from the IRS. Employers must also pay contributions to cover retroactive increases in benefits and make up any investment losses by the fund. In Defined Contribution Plans, the employer must pay the amount specified in the plan. Under Defined Benefit Plans, if the company fails to make required payments, it may be assessed a penalty unless it is given a waiver. If a waiver is granted, participants in the plan must be notified. Under some circumstances, the plan may have a legal claim against the company's assets or the employer may have to provide security to cover the unfunded portion. Single-employer plans must notify participants if the employer fails to meet minimum funding payments.[11]

Some plans may be top-heavy, that is, they favor older workers with longer service and higher pay. Other plans give more weight to the age of the worker, in addition to the number of years of service. A worker who puts in 10 years from age 45 to 55 may get greater benefits than the person who works 10 years from age 30 to 40. This method of calculating benefits is sometimes called the fractional rule. Higher paid workers may be favored when their plans give more benefits above a specific dollar amount of income.

If the plan becomes so top-heavy that 60 percent of the money put into the plan or paid as benefits goes to company officers or owners, the plan may be required to balance this inequity by adding 3 percent of pay to lower-paid workers, or giving them an increased benefit of 2 percent for each of their first 10 years of work.[12] Discuss this element with your plan administrator.

Protection for Your Plan
Most private sector Defined Benefit Plans are insured by the PBGC, but *excluded* from this insurance coverage by ERISA are

- Defined Contribution Plans.
- Some Defined Benefit Plans, including federal, state and local government plans, some church and fraternal plans.
- Professional service employers' plans (doctors, lawyers, etc.) that do not cover more than 25 active participants at any one time. These plans are likely to be heavily populated by women because they include many care-giving and nurturing career choices.

- Plans maintained outside the United States primarily for non-resident aliens.
- Workers' compensation and unemployment insurance.
- Non-tax-qualified plans (plans that are not eligible for favorable tax status under the Internal Revenue Code).
- Plans not funded with employer contributions.[13]

PBGC provides insurance when a plan under its coverage is terminated, and it will become the trustee for that plan. It will pay the retiree up to the maximum allowed by law (in 1989, $2,028.41 per month for a single-employer retiree who retired at age 65 with no survivor benefits). Some extra benefits in a plan may not be insured by PBGC. These might include severance pay, lump-sum death benefits, and some types of disability pay. PBGC does pay survivor benefits. If a plan is terminated before a worker retires, survivor benefits are paid by PBGC.[14] To determine if your plan is covered by PBGC, ask your plan administrator, check the Summary Plan Description, or write PBGC, 2020 "K" St., N.W., Washington, DC 20006-1806.

Easy Action List

- Check if your plan is covered by PBGC.
- Find out if your plan offers benefits other than a retirement pension, such as disability coverage.

Pension plans are initiated by employers on a voluntary basis. Businesses are not legally required to have a plan, although competition for qualified employees and federal tax advantages motivate many employers to initiate a plan.

Plans may be terminated in the standard way, when the plan has enough assets to pay all benefit liabilities. In this case, PBGC oversees as the plan administrator purchases annuities, usually from insurance companies. The workers receive appropriate notification, and payments are made routinely. A plan may also be terminated in distress. Here, the employer has met one of the following four criteria:

- Chapter 7 bankruptcy.
- Chapter 11 bankruptcy reorganization.
- PBGC determines the employer cannot pay its debts and cannot continue in business.
- PBGC determines that, solely due to a decline in the employer's workforce, pension costs have become unreasonably burdensome.

In a distress termination, PBGC calculates the amount of the promised benefits that can actually be paid and compares that amount to the PBGC guarantee. If it exceeds the guarantee, the plan administrator pays as if it were a standard termination. If not, PBGC pays the difference to reach the guaranteed amount. It uses insurance funds to pay the unfunded liability.[15]

Rule Number 6: Know Your Plan

It is never too soon to begin gathering facts about your pension plan. The 17-step questionnaire/checklist below can help you put together the information you need to make intelligent retirement decisions.

1. My pension plan is a:
   Defined Benefit Plan _____
   Defined Contribution Plan _____
2. My Plan Administrator is
   Name: _____
   Phone: _____
   Address: _____
   _____
3. I have received my Summary Plan Description. _____
4. I have received my Annual Report. _____
5. I have received my Survivor's Benefit Information. _____
6. I am now fully vested _____
   or I will be fully vested in _____ years.
7. I have _____ years of service in my plan.

8. Will I receive a lump-sum payment upon retirement, or will I receive monthly payments for life? _____

9. Will my Social Security affect my pension benefit? _____

10. I can retire with full benefits at age _____

11. Will my spouse be covered by my pension? _____

12. Are my benefits insured by PBGC? _____

13. If I want to go back to work either full-time or part-time after I retire, will my pension change? _____

14. What happens to the balance of my contributions if I die, either before retirement or after? _____
    _____

15. Does my plan have an early retirement provision? _____

16. A full year of service equals _____ hours in paid status.

17. What is the best time for me to retire in terms of dollar benefits? _____

Ask questions and keep asking until you are satisfied with the answers. Learn your rights. The American Association of Retired Persons (AARP) publishes many helpful brochures, two of which are

- Protect Yourself—A Woman's Guide to Pension Rights (D12258)
- Guide to Understanding Your Pension Plan (D13533)

The brochures are free. Write to AARP Fulfillment (DD057), 1909 "K" St., N.W., Washington, DC 20049. Include the catalog number, given in parentheses above, and allow six to eight weeks for delivery.

Withdrawal of Funds from Other Plans
Your own savings can be another resource beyond your employer's pension plan. If you have paid into tax-deferred savings, be aware that the withdrawal rules are similar to those of your pension plan. You have the choice of withdrawing your money on a regular basis, called annuitizing. The amount is usually determined by a formula of so many dollars per month per thousand you have on deposit. *But* if you

choose this method, and you should die before your contributions are exhausted, the balance in your account goes to the company, and not to your heirs or estate.

The other choice you have for withdrawal is called randomizing. In this method, you randomly withdraw different sums upon request, perhaps $5,000 this June and $7,500 next September. You can instruct a mutual fund to pay a specified amount per month, using the principal when not enough dividends are present to cover the amount named. If you should die before your funds are depleted, the balance will go to your beneficiary or estate. But when your contributions and interest are gone, there will be no more money for you.

With the annuitized method, you get more than you paid in if you live a long, long time; and with the randomized system, you are sure that you and/or your beneficiary will get all your money back. A tough choice, but you can hedge your bet by having more than one account. Randomize one and annuitize the other.

Rule Number 7:   Investigate the Pay-Out Rules Where You Have Tax-Deferred Savings

If requirements are not to your liking, all is not lost. You can roll over your account by transferring it to another company whose regulations are more appropriate. Your financial adviser, banker, CPA or planner can help make the shift.

Pension plans are an important element of your retirement plan. Your company plan, personal savings, and insurance policies should provide a powerful combination to give you the necessary financial foundation for your golden years.

Endnotes

1. *Your Pension: Things You Should Know About Your Pension Plan,* (Washington, DC: Pension Benefit Guaranty Corporation), p. 3.

2. Ibid., p. 3.

3. Ibid., p. 2.

4. Ibid., p. 2.

5. Ibid., p. 5.

6. Ibid., p. 5.

7. Ibid., p. 6.

8. Ibid., p. 8.

9. Ibid., p. 11

10. Ibid., p. 14.

11. Ibid., p. 15.

12. Reid, Heddy F., ed. *A Guide to Understanding Your Pension Plan: A Pension Handbook*, National Pension Assistance Project, p. 18.

13. *Your Pension: Things You Should Know About Your Pension Plan*, op. cit., p. 16.

14. Ibid., p. 17.

15. Ibid., p. 19.

Planning Chart—Chapter 6

Your age now:

20s	30s	40s	50s
Know the details of your employer's pension plan	Same	Same	Same
Keep the requirements of a pension plan in mind as you change jobs	Same	Same	Same
Know the details of your spouse's plan, and who the beneficiary is	Same	Same	Same
	Discuss with spouse plans for both of you, keeping each plan seperate	Same	Same
	Diversify retirement holdings	Same	Same

Starting Your Own Plan
—The First Easy Step

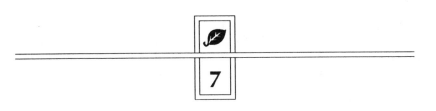

The importance of setting retirement goals cannot be overemphasized. Most people understand the need to create and set goals, just as they recognize the importance of establishing and following a budget. Few of us, even with the best intentions, follow through.

To be successful in reaching your goals, it is important to recognize the resistance you probably have toward maintaining a plan. If you experiment with the following sentence stems, you will begin to understand why you are resisting.

- The bad thing about setting goals is. . .
- If I followed my plan I. . .
- The good thing about not reaching my goals is. . .
- If I achieved the goals I set. . .
- At the thought of setting goals. . .

Work from the goal back to the present to develop your strategy. Corporate salespersons are frequently assigned a yearly quota or target. That quota is then broken down into semiannual, quarterly, and monthly goals, along with daily activities designed to reach the goals. Regular meetings with the sales manager track the sales representative's progress. You may want to adapt this procedure to achieve your goals.

Tami M. did this to fulfill a personal goal. She had always wanted to employ an image consultant who would also be her personal shopper for a new wardrobe. She read books, talked to friends, and interviewed consultants until she found the right one. She wanted to spend $3,000 a year on new clothes and learned the consultant's fee would be $200. Tami's goal was to save approximately $250 a month for a year.

Set a goal that is workable for you. If the standard is set too high, you may become overwhelmed and feel defeated at the beginning. The initial burst of enthusiasm and interest can be a helpful boost to sustain your commitment.

Easy Action List

- Think of one major goal you reached in your lifetime.
- Identify two small goals you will meet during the next month.

Once you have determined your desired result, have established a time frame, and understand what is required on a daily basis to reach that goal, you must then decide if the goal is worth the price required. In other words, what are you willing to do to get what you want? The process itself is important. Each goal should be broken down into achievable sub- or intermediate goals. Each individual achievement is a cause for celebration, and will keep your energy and motivation high.

To continue with our shopping scenario, Tami had to reexamine her budget to find an extra $250 a month. She had to weigh the shopping trip against other activities she enjoyed. She also thought about new ways she could earn money.

As you review your progress, adjust or fine-tune your behavior to guarantee results. If after two months, Tami had not saved any money, she could have decreased the amount of money or increased the time frame. She could have simply gone shopping with a friend instead of hiring a consultant. Tami might have adjusted her strategy in ways that would have allowed her to accomplish the goal, change goals, or abandon the project.

Unforeseen complications and temptations can result in an internal struggle. You must review what you are willing to do to get what you want. Make a conscious decision; do not let the choice be made by default, which is a passive reaction. Sometimes women are pulled in many different directions by responsibilities and obligations and must struggle to achieve a sense of balance. You are more likely to maintain a sense of control if you set your own personal and professional goals. Define general areas and then address them individually. You might compose a list of general areas such as:

- Relationships
- Health
- Spiritual issues
- Financial needs
- Professional growth

Set goals within each area you want to change. Start with just one goal and, as you become comfortable in that area, move on to another. You might use these general guidelines when setting goals:

Set a concrete and measurable goal.
Know exactly what you want. For example, you may want to invest money in a mutual fund but have no experience with investing and feel uncomfortable or even intimidated by finance and investments. Define your goal specifically: I want to select a blue-chip mutual fund that has shown steady growth and invest $500 in it. To select an appropriate mutual fund, you would have to read about mutual funds in magazines, talk to friends and financial consultants, and read the prospectus and other information supplied by the mutual fund.

That seems like a lot to do, but it will be easier if you set subgoals as stepping stones along the way. Your subgoals in this example might be:

- I will read at least three issues of a financial magazine such as *Changing Times* or *Money*.
- I will talk to two friends who have invested in mutual funds.
- I will talk to two financial advisers and/or attend a seminar regarding mutual funds.

Establish a realistic time frame.
Put some realistic time constraints on what you want to do. It doesn't have to be done tomorrow, but give yourself a limit and stick to it. Your goal now will read: I will select a appropriate blue-chip mutual fund and invest $500 within six months. I will read at least one financial magazine for each of three months. In the next three months, I will talk to three friends and two financial consultants about blue-chip mutual funds.

Easy Action List

- Set one goal to accomplish within six months.
- Use the forms provided here in Exhibits 7-1 and 7-2, or create your own.

Determine an evaluation method.
You should keep track of your progress. If you schedule time for your goals as you schedule other activities, you make a pact with yourself to do the tasks you want done. Mark your schedule book in advance to go to the library to read a financial magazine or purchase one at the newsstand on a specific day. Schedule reading time by blocking out one hour on three or four different days during the month. As you accomplish your goal, mark it boldly on your tracking sheet.

Review progress on a regular (weekly or daily) basis.
Refine your behavior so that you are working toward your goal in the most efficient and effective manner. The time you save can be applied toward something else you want.

Exhibit 7–1

Priorities Chart

Suggested Categories:

Career	Health	Leisure/Recreation
Education	Personal	Relationship
Financial	Social	Religious/Spiritual

Rank			
1			
2			
3			
4			
5			

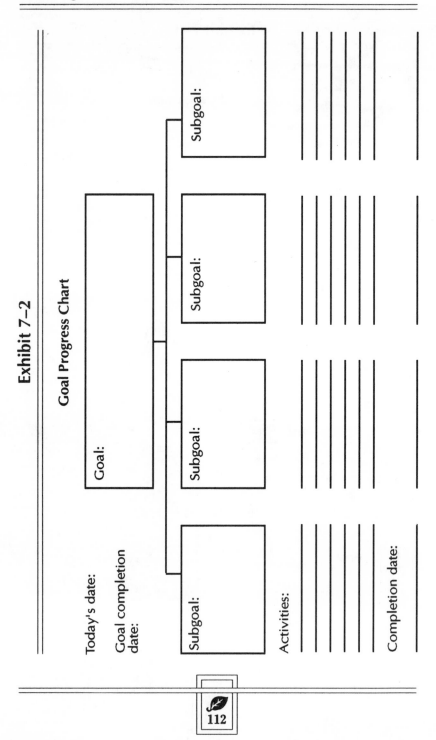

Exhibit 7–2

Goal Progress Chart

Today's date:

Goal completion date:

Goal:

Subgoal:

Subgoal:

Subgoal:

Subgoal:

Activities:

Completion date:

Give yourself credit.
Pat yourself on the back. Perhaps this feels uncomfortable to you. But giving yourself credit is an important part of getting things done.

If your goals are specific, measurable, attainable, right for you, and set within a realistic time frame, you'll have a greater chance of meeting them. If you find yourself unable to stick with a goal-oriented program, explore your feelings regarding the goal you have set for yourself. Common forms of financial sabotage include the two extremes of under- and over-spending, which can indicate emotional conflicts. Research shows that recently divorced women often spend lavishly because they no longer feel worthy and may use buying something to brighten their spirits. At the other extreme, some women are so frightened about never being able to make ends meet that they force themselves to live uncomfortably.

This was the case with Marie F., a college math professor for more than 15 years. She had worked hard, saved her money, and was able to purchase several pieces of rental property. Most of the properties had appreciated in value and were bringing in almost enough income to cover their expenses. She found herself dreading work and longed to quit teaching to begin another career. She believed she was trapped in her job, even though she had ample financial resources. She was unable to resign and live on income from the sale of one or two of her properties because she didn't trust her personal resourcefulness or her ability to get another job if she should change her mind. Instead of using her assets to make her life better, she limited both her options and herself.

Michelle V. is at the other extreme. When she was a young girl, both her parents worked outside the home. They spent relatively little time with Michelle but would buy her a new toy weekly. As she grew older, she would purchase something new whenever she felt lonely and discouraged; consequently, she found herself dangerously in debt. The relief that she felt from making purchases lasted only a short time, while the reality of overdue notices became a new area of stress in her life.

Terri M. had been raised during the depression years. She frequently heard her parents talk about their sacrifices. No matter how much

Lois was on her lunch hour. Seated in a diner near her office, she ordered a diet plate and decaf. She had worked for the same doctor for a number of years as the receptionist, bookkeeper, and, as she put it, "Great Mother Hen to everyone."

After some serious thought, Lois said, "Every woman needs a bank account of her own. If her husband should die suddenly, as mine did, she would have a source of cash without any hassle. It took me a year and a half to get the house in my name." After the bills were paid from her husband's long illness, she was left with the house and little more. She returned to the workforce at the same level she left it when they got married. She has never advanced. A few times she has considered attending classes to expand her skills, but she never seems to get around to it.

money Terri saved, she never felt she had enough and felt guilty whenever she purchased something for herself. She had completely internalized the belief that life is hard, an image that does not include the use of money for pleasure or comfort.

These women exemplify some of the emotional baggage that we can carry with respect to money and financial matters in general. In part, choosing your future may involve understanding some of these types of connections in your own life. Once you understand some of these influences, think about the things you *really* want.

Your Financial Goals

You have now determined your net worth and your spending habits and have even thought about influences in your life that may distort your decision-making process. The next step is to explore your financial goals. You can organize your thoughts into three time frames. Determine what you want financially during the next year or two, within five to ten years, and then after that. None of these goals are engraved in stone. They can be changed as you choose.

Choices will be inherent in this process. When you save or invest for intermediate or long-term goals, you postpone immediate wants. Long-range goals will never materialize if you always give in to immediate gratification. A balance you can live with and feel happy about is essential. Generally, you can find balance only through trial and error.

Be specific as you set your financial goals. Define what financial independence means for you in dollars and cents instead of using a vague phrase. Financial independence is the ability to live off your investments and work for pay only when you are interested. Know exactly what that means and write it down. Unfortunately, the impact of taxes and inflation must be figured in.

Rule Number 1:   Goals Are The Key

The purpose of writing your goals is to convert your dreams into a workable set of realistic and achievable aims. Use the following worksheet (shown in Exhibit 7-3) to help determine your retirement needs.

Exhibit 7–3

Projected Retirement Cash Flow
Example of Widow Age 65

	Yourself	Spouse	Combined
Social Security	$ 10,200	$	$
Pension plan	24,000		
Profit sharing			
IRA/Keogh			
Other			
Total estimated annual income			$ 34,200

Less expenses:

	Yourself		
Food	$ 1,800	Clothing	1,000
Transportation	2,400	Medical	2,400
Home maintenance	1,000	Insur. prem.	600
Utilities	1,200	Personal	800
Mortgage interest	12,000	Other	
		Total expenses:	$

Less taxes:

Federal	$ 8,000
State	2,000
Other	1,000

Total taxes	$ 11,800
Total outgo	$ 34,200
Net cash flow (income minus outgo)	$

A great deal of importance rests on the realistic completion of this worksheet. Take time to prepare it as accurately as you can and update it frequently as conditions change. Because this worksheet does not factor in inflation, it is most useful for women nearing retirement.

The first step is to estimate how much you will be receiving annually from the retirement vehicles you already have: that is, Social Security, your pension plan, etc. Now estimate (in today's dollars) what your expenses would be. Clearly where and how you choose to live will have a big impact on these estimates. You might want to make an estimate for each of the lifestyles of interest to you. How much would it cost to live in a mobile home year-round and travel around the country? Or how much would it cost to move to a condo in town and have a more active lifestyle? What about if you just wanted to maintain your current lifestyle? What would that cost? Base your estimates on a full year. Don't forget taxes.

Now for each alternative, calculate net cash flow—that is, the amount of money per year you need to have saved to support that lifestyle. Each of these annual net cash flow figures represents one of your alternative goals. In order to live that lifestyle, you're going to need roughly that number multiplied by a number of years.

Some people prefer to save a long time to take a special vacation. Others elect to take smaller, less expensive trips throughout the year. Only you can know if what you want is worth the cost. The basic question is: What do I want and what am I willing to do to get it?

Rule Number 2:   Start Now

Three factors, money, time and investment return, are interrelated. More time exists for the interest to compound on your money if you are young. You can start with less money and tolerate a lower return. By contrast, if you start saving later in life, you must save more each year or get a higher return on your money to arrive at the same result. This underlines the need to begin saving early, even if you can afford to save only a small amount.

The compound interest tables shown in Exhibits 7-4 and 7-5 will give you a better idea of how your savings now can grow for retirement use later.

Exhibit 7–4

Compound Interest Table
$100 Monthly Principal (Deposit made at the beginning of each month)

Rate	5 Years	10 Years	15 Years	20 Years	25 Years	30 years
5%	$6,809	$15,499	$26,590	$40,746	$58,812	$81,870
6%	6,982	16,326	28,831	45,565	67,958	97,926
7%	7,160	17,202	31,286	51,041	78,747	117,606
8%	7,341	18,128	33,976	57,266	91,484	141,761
9%	7,527	19,109	36,928	64,346	106,531	171,468
10%	7,717	20,146	40,162	72,399	124,316	207,929
11%	7,912	21,243	43,707	81,561	145,346	252,828
12%	8,110	22,404	47,593	91,986	170,221	308,097
13%	8,314	24,631	51,852	103,849	199,648	376,152
14%	8,522	24,929	56,520	117,347	234,464	459,962
15%	8,734	26,302	61,637	132,707	275,656	563,177

Exhibit 7-5

Compound Interest Table
$100 Quarterly Principal (Deposit made at the beginning of each quarter)

Rate	5 Years	10 Years	15 Years	20 Years	25 Years	30 years
5%	$2,279	$5,187	$8,900	$13,637	$19,684	$27,401
6%	2,339	5,469	9,657	15,262	22,764	32,801
7%	2,400	5,766	10,488	17,110	26,397	39,421
8%	2,463	6,082	11,399	19,211	30,690	47,557
9%	2,527	6,415	12,398	21,603	35,766	57,557
10%	2,593	6,769	13,494	24,325	41,768	69,861
11%	2,660	7,143	14,696	27,424	48,871	85,010
12%	2,729	7,539	16,014	30,952	57,277	103,671
13%	2,800	7,957	17,460	34,969	67,228	126,663
14%	2,872	8,401	19,046	39,544	79,010	154,998
15%	2,945	8,870	20,785	44,752	92,958	189,916

The Rule of 72 can be useful when you select specific dollar amounts needed and when setting a time schedule. Divide 72 by the amount of interest, or the return you will earn on your investment. The quotient will tell you the amount of time needed to double your money. For example, if you receive a return of 10 percent, you will double your money in 7.2 years (72 divided by 10 = 7.2). A return of 12 percent will double your money in six years, whereas a return of 6 percent will double your money in twelve years.

Long-established advice is "pay yourself first" and save at least 10 percent of income, not an easy task for many people. The main objective is to make saving as effortless as possible, and to cause withdrawal from savings to be painful.

Rule of 72

72	÷	Interest Rate	=	Years to Double Money
72	÷	12	=	6.0
72	÷	10	=	7.2
72	÷	8	=	9.0
72	÷	6	=	12.0

Easy Action List

- Get started.
- Save all or part of any new disposable income.
- Use past financial decisions to evaluate current practices for appropriateness.

Procrastination is dangerous. It is easy to believe you will begin to save as soon as an item is paid off, when the kids have everything they need, or when college costs have been paid. The right time for saving rarely arrives, but the habit and discipline of saving is as important as the amount saved. Once begun, the magic of compounding interest works for you. Ten dollars a month can make a difference (see Exhibit 7-6). Start now.

Take advantage of a company savings plan. As discussed in Chapter 6, these plans, called deferred compensation, 401(k), or tax-sheltered annuities, permit money to be saved from pay before it is taxed. The money compounds tax-deferred until you are 59-1/2 years old, although you are not required to begin withdrawals from these types of accounts until age 70-1/2.

Instruct employers to put the money into a bank, credit union, or other savings institution to make your money more accessible. Once you have a nest egg, invest in a certificate of deposit to resist using the money. A certificate of deposit is a savings account with a bank or savings and loan in which you invest the money for a specific time period at an interest rate higher than a regular savings account. If you withdraw the money before the time period has expired, an interest

Exhibit 7–6

How Ten Dollars Per Month Will Grow

This table can be used to find out how long it will take to reach your financial goals. It shows the growth of monthly $10 deposits invested at various interest rates. Put aside $10 a month for five years at 10 percent, for example, and you'll have $781—the figure at the intersection of the year five and 10 percent interest columns. If you can invest $50 each month, you will have five times $781, or $3,905, in five years.

Year	Interest Rate			
	5.25%	7%	8%	10%
1	$123	$124	$125	$127
3	389	399	408	421
5	685	716	740	781
8	1,190	1,283	1,348	1,474
10	1,842	1,733	1,842	2,066
20	4,237	5,222	5,929	7,657
25	6,193	8,126	9,574	11,295

penalty will be charged. Use that penalty as a deterrent to spending it before other resources are exhausted.

Another good rule is that when you receive a raise or pay off a car, credit cards, or other loans, you should save all or part of the new disposable income. You can also use past financial decisions to evaluate whether current practices are appropriate. As you build your assets and your children leave home, for example, you may want to revise the amount of life insurance you own. An obvious and important step is to review bank and credit card statements to check for accuracy. Be assertive about correcting problems. Credit card companies and banks have clearly defined instructions to help you resolve conflicts. And perhaps the most basic and useful advice is to examine your spending habits periodically to be as careful as you can.

Easy Action List

- Put idle cash to work. Convert old traveler's checks or cash into an interest-bearing savings account.

- Carry fewer credit cards that charge annual fees. Select only those that offer you the best terms. The interest rate is not as important as the yearly fees when the balance is paid monthly. If you carry a balance, shop for the lowest interest rates.

- Examine your loans. Consumer credit has lost its tax advantage, which increases the cost of your loan. If you own a home, consider a tax-deductible home equity loan to pay off other debts. Do not, however, use the money to pay off low-interest loans such as student loans. Use that cash for an investment that can bring you a higher return.

- Pay bills at the last minute from an interest-bearing checking account. You may choose to put your paycheck into a savings account and transfer money to the checking account once or twice a month to pay bills. To avoid having unpaid bills around, write the checks immediately, and put the due date on the envelope where the stamp normally goes. Stamp and mail the bill on the designated date.

- Adjust your income tax withholding so you come out even at the end of the tax year. Most people enjoy looking forward to a tax refund because it feels like a gift. A refund means you have lent money interest-free to the government. Pay yourself instead, and allow that interest to compound in your account.

- Sell or give away unused items. Hold garage sales for unused items and save the proceeds.

- Examine all insurance policies. Most premiums can be reduced by increasing the amount of the deductible you pay. If you have mortgage insurance, you might find term insurance less expensive.

Rule Number 3:   Control Your Most Important Resource—Your Time

You may feel pulled in so many different directions that very little time is left for personal pleasures and regeneration. The paradox is that without that special time devoted to yourself, you will ultimately face the problems of fatigue, burnout, or an unbalanced life.

That is what happened to Sally R. For many years, she was an overachiever. She spent almost all of her waking hours climbing the corporate ladder. She accused her husband of selfishness because he wanted to spend time with her when she had a project due. She convinced herself that her husband was holding her back from greater successes, and she filed for divorce. Once alone, she had more time to pursue her business activities. She made some time for friends, and had enough money to afford many luxuries of life, but she was often depressed and spent time and money on psychotherapy.

One day she learned she had an illness that necessitated an operation and ten days away from work. She had never before been out of the office without calling in for messages. For most of the ten days, Sally

Irene was a hard-working woman, and she learned over the years to make every action count. She raised four children alone, and each is accomplishing a great deal in her or his field. They learned how to work with others and how to be at peace with themselves from their mother.

Irene leaned across the arm of her chair and said, "I think the biggest question at retirement time is 'Who am I and what do I want?' Of course, who you are determines a great deal of what you want."

She had worked in the same building at a large university for 30 years; the library was more than her working home, it was her identity.

"Yes, there are disappointments. Some people smile, but don't mean it; some people make promises, but don't keep them. I have seen it all, and what helped me most was the spiritual side. I meditate and use self-control through my mind."

Irene retired a total of five times. After she left the library, she went into business. She eventually sold the business and went on to professional positions. Presently she is working in a senior citizens center.

"You must set goals; you may never reach them, but it is so much fun trying, and you do so many new things on the way." She does not recommend doing the same thing you did before, but instead to try new fields. She hasn't been surprised by retirement because she is so busy living day-to-day. She mentioned that the only surprise is how easy it is to get tunnel vision.

"It's extremely important to keep contributing. After two or three weeks of resting, if nothing is happening, I am not happy. I am not contributing. There's so much to be done."

left the office problems for her secretary to handle. She spent her time sleeping, reading fiction, and visiting with friends. She found herself in better spirits than ever before, although her illness was a serious one. When she returned to work, many people told Sally that she looked better than usual. The comment was made so often, she was forced to discover what was different. She concluded that for the first time in years she was completely rested. Her level of depression had directly corresponded to her fatigue. When troubled, Sally rarely slept through the night, and became so accustomed to fatigue that she no longer labeled it as a problem. The experience was an important lesson for her. Now, when she finds her spirits falling, she makes sure she takes a little extra time to relax.

Fatigue and burnout are important issues for many women today. To avoid them, you might follow these six steps:

- Get in touch with your body. Know when you are tired. Pay attention to the messages you receive. When you are tired, rest. Rearrange your schedule and your priorities to allow time for that rest. It is not necessary to do everything by yourself. Explore ways to share cooking, driving, and cleaning responsibilities. Hire out work that you can afford to have done by someone else.

- Take care of yourself emotionally and physically. It is okay to admit you might benefit from the expertise of another person. Ask for help and enlist the aid of a psychologist or psychotherapist. Many professionals work at clinics and/or accept fees on an ability to pay basis. Or use your library to find self-help books.

- Eat and exercise well. Recipe books with nutritionally sound recipes are available for today's busy woman. Regular exercise requires a small investment of time for a big return. Be aware of the need for and benefits from exercise and try to incorporate more opportunities for movement into your life.

- Do not take care of everyone else. You cannot be mother to the entire world. Husbands and children can be responsible for some of their own needs and may be happier being so.

- Develop your sense of humor. Notice how humor helps reduce the intensity of a serious event in your life.
- Remind yourself that the world will not end if a specific project is not accomplished.

Use your time as fully as possible for yourself. Women often have only short periods of time to work without interruption. Remember, in five minutes you can:

- Review your to-do list
- Make an appointment
- Write a short note
- Make out a grocery list
- Plan menus for a week

In ten minutes you can:

- Call a friend to resume a good relationship
- Arrange childcare for an evening out
- Clean out a desk or drawer
- Do some toning exercises
- Plan your reading material for the weekend

In half an hour you can:

- Do exercises
- Prepare a meal to freeze and serve later
- Read articles you have been neglecting
- Meditate
- Plan your next project

The point is to make the fullest use possible of the time available.

If procrastination is a problem for you, try to break down projects into very small parts and then work on one particular part without feeling overwhelmed about the entire project. Explore the benefits you might receive from putting things off. The following sentence stems might guide you in your understanding:

- The good thing about not starting. . .
- At the thought of doing things in a timely manner. . .
- The good thing about starting but not finishing is. . .

Sarah B. is a highly organized woman who seems able to balance many demands. She attributes her success to making a list of things to do and then ranking the list in terms of importance. She never begins a less important task unless the other more urgent jobs have been completed. To earn money for college, Sarah worked on a factory assembly line. Her income was directly linked to her production, which caused her to examine every movement until she streamlined the task. She has carried that habit into her present life. She automatically reviews her movements to make sure she is efficient and effective, which is especially important for jobs that are done on a regular basis. Those jobs should be done quickly without sacrificing quality, so you can move on to something else.

Learn to delegate. Many women find it easier to do things themselves and avoid the hassle of encouraging others to do their share. Meet with the family and divide household duties on a rotating basis. You might even use a chart similar to the one that follows. When someone does not complete the task, leave it undone. You are helping someone to be irresponsible when you do the task instead.

Job Chart

Week of:

Job	Person	Day 1	2	3	4	5	6	7
Wash dishes	Jill							
Set table	John							
Laundry	Mike							
Clean bathroom	Alice							
Clean livingroom	Jill							

Creating Your Own Future

If you set priorities and adjust your goals, you will feel you are saving for a specific reason rather than depriving yourself of some temporary pleasure. Goals help you achieve what you want only when you define exactly what you want.

Understand your relationship to money and how you use it. The information and exercises included in this chapter will help you start that process, but it is not something you can do overnight. Take time to complete the process and to think about your results and your reactions. Then you will have laid the foundation for financial independence.

Planning Chart—Chapter 7

Your age now:

20s	30s	40s	50s
Establish goals: professional growth health	Update goals, develop method to evaluate	Same	Same
Start savings plan	Continue	Evaluate, diversify	Same
Find new or hidden cash	Continue	Continue	Same

Nothing Ventured, Nothing Gained
—Risk and Investments

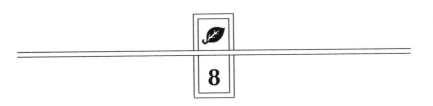

8

It is time to decide how to invest the money you have saved. Everyone would like to have a safe and risk-free investment, but each investment has some risk associated with it. The type and the amount of risk is related to the investment choice. Investments can be divided into two categories: equity or fixed. Examples of an equity, or ownership, investment include real estate, stocks, mutual funds and collectibles. The good news about owning something is that you enjoy a profit when the investment appreciates. But should the investment decrease in value, you, as the owner, must suffer the decline as well. This type of risk, loss of principal, is involved with owning virtually any investment that fluctuates in value.

The other broad investment option is to lend your money with the assurance that you will be paid a certain interest rate for the use of your money (fixed or debt money). When you put money into a savings account, certificate of deposit, Treasury Bill, or a bond that you hold until maturity, you know the return on your investment in advance. The risk for this type of investment involves the loss or erosion of your purchasing power.

Although you receive a predetermined return on your investment, inflation and your tax rate will decide your actual return. The higher the inflation rate or the tax rate, the lower your return.

Easy Action List

- List all your equity money.
- List all your fixed money.
- Check your tax rate from last year's income tax return.
- Find the current inflation rate (often reported in newspapers).

Most people are acutely aware of loss-of-principal risk and often shy away from equity investments. Jan R. avoided the risk by investing her entire savings in certificates of deposit at various banks. She liked seeing the interest increase. She shopped around to get the highest yield whenever a deposit came due. Unfortunately, Jan didn't take taxes or inflation into consideration. With an 8 percent return, approximately one third of that, or almost 2.5 percent, went to pay taxes. She was left with an after-tax return of 5.6 percent. Assuming inflation hovered about five percent, she was only slightly ahead of a break-even point. If inflation had risen during the time her money was locked in, she would have lost money, just as if she had invested in a stock that had declined in value.

Your challenge is to decide on a balance between the two risks. With equity money risk you have the opportunity to enjoy a return that can be substantially higher than inflation and your tax rate, but you also have the possibility of losing some of the principal—the money you actually invested. By contrast, with fixed money risk, you will get back the money you invested as well as some return. The risk lies in whether that amount will keep you ahead of taxes and inflation.

The risk of losing money in an equity investment (stocks, real estate) is more obvious than losing money in a debt (bonds) investment. With an equity investment, you can actually end up with less money than you began with. With a fixed-dollar investment, it may appear that you have made money, because you have more at the end of the time period than when you began. The loss is in the erosion of purchasing power, which is a more subtle loss but is a loss, nonetheless.

Risk-taking, particularly financial risk-taking, is often difficult at first. Those who inherit stocks, for example, often hold them, even though the investment may be inappropriate, rather than face a new decision. Remember that the difference between risk-taking and gambling is education. Education helps reduce fear and enables women to take greater risks without as much anxiety.

Use some of the following sentence stems to explore your feelings surrounding money and risk:

- At the thought of losing money, I. . .
- If I choose the wrong investment, I will. . .
- When it comes to making financial choices, I never. . .
- Putting money in the bank makes me. . .

Several years ago, Betty K. was divorced. She was a salesperson for a copier company and happened to call on an accounting firm. When talking to the accountant, the conversation changed from copiers to savings accounts. Betty admitted that her $3,000 savings was in a regular savings account at a local bank. The accountant suggested she move her money to a much higher-paying money market account and gave her a copy of a magazine article listing names and addresses of several firms. Betty transferred all but $500 to a money market fund located across the country. However, she frequently woke up in the middle of the night, worrying about her money, because she didn't really understand how money market funds worked. When she received written confirmation that her money had been invested in the fund, she wrote back to ask for a full redemption. Since the fund was paying much higher interest than her savings account, Betty was excited to receive a check including interest on her money after such a short time. She was also reassured that she was able to receive her money promptly, without any difficulty. Betty then began reading articles on money market funds and paid more attention to news stories about them. She soon decided to return her money to the same fund and this time was far more comfortable with her decision.

People who have developed wealth over the years usually have taken some risks. They opened their own businesses, invested in equities, and reinvested their earnings. When you take risks, you must stretch your comfort zone. The first step is the most difficult. Many people report that buying their first home was an anxiety-ridden decision, because the financial commitment was often the largest one they had ever made. Once comfortable with that decision, they were able to make other choices.

Rule Number 1:   Talk to Successful Risk-Takers

Join organizations and groups that enable you to mingle with people you admire and would like to know. If you feel shy about talking to someone more accomplished, a good opener might be to ask them what they consider to be their greatest professional accomplishment. People are often flattered to talk about their successes and will make time for you even though they are busy.

You also might find a person who has acquired wealth in ways that interest you. Perhaps they invest in stocks or own rental properties. By talking to others who are more knowledgeable, you can develop your knowledge and understanding of investment strategies you might be able to use.

Nancy T. had found a used car she wanted to purchase and was shopping lending institutions for the best interest rate. One day she heard a business associate bragging about the interest rate she had negotiated. Nancy had never realized loan rates varied for different people at the *same* bank. She established the rate she wanted to pay and approached several banks before she achieved her goal. In the process she developed her negotiating skills and became less intimidated by bankers.

Rule Number 2:   Read and Educate Yourself

Money is a topic that interests many people. Newspapers generally contain several pages or an entire section devoted to business. Entire magazines are devoted to how to make and invest money. Inexpensive classes and courses are offered through colleges and organizations. Make it a high priority to attend, and familiarize yourself with the jargon. The first time you read a magazine or newspaper article, it may not make much sense. Soon the words will repeat themselves and you will understand more with each reading.

Rule Number 3:   Do Your Homework

If you are interested in a particular investment, learn about it by reading and talking to knowledgeable people. Investigate the company, and do not rely entirely on the recommendation of a single person. Other people have their own biases and risk tolerance levels. What might be comfortable for another person might cause you sleepless nights. Keep a file of the material you accumulate.

Rule Number 4:   Experiment and Practice

When you begin to invest, start small. Keep track of the investment's performance. If you make a mistake, make a note of it and do not repeat it. View each mistake as a learning tool and a way of redefining your course or your goals.

Rule Number 5:   Invest

Thinking about an investment will not bring you financial returns. After studying the field, take the risk, and regularly evaluate whether you want to continue on that course or adjust it.

All investments have risk; nothing is completely risk-free. If you put your money under the mattress, the house could burn down.

To balance the need for safety against the need for growth to keep ahead of taxes and inflation, many people subscribe to the pyramid style of investing (see Exhibit 8-1). The base of the pyramid is the solid foundation money. This would include your emergency cash reserve, disability insurance, and life insurance. Once those financial obligations have been met, the next step is to make other investments. Many authorities see the potential loss of principal as a greater risk than the erosion of spending power that results from inflation and suggest you invest money first in the fixed-dollar segment before investing in the owned-dollar category. The younger you are, the more inflation will affect your investment dollars and the more you need to counter the impact of inflation by investing in vehicles that have the possibility to outpace inflation.

Traditionally, second-tier investments include those where the principal remains steady and the interest rate can vary. The most common example of such an investment is a certificate of deposit. The bank, as a member of the Federal Deposit Insurance Corporation (FDIC), guarantees that the principal will remain intact and that the interest rate is locked in for a specific period.

Exhibit 8–1

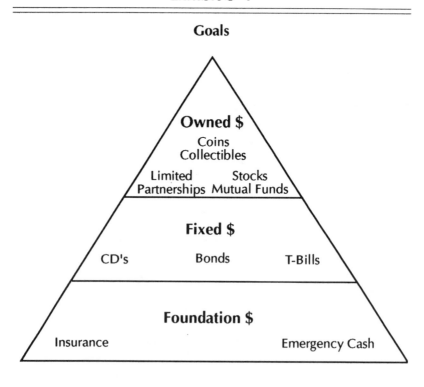

Goals

Owned $
Coins
Collectibles
Limited   Stocks
Partnerships Mutual Funds

Fixed $

CD's   Bonds   T-Bills

Foundation $

Insurance   Emergency Cash

The next risk level would include more stable income stocks and mutual funds, such as utility stocks and high-quality corporate stocks that pay dividends. Real estate investments might come next, along with other stocks. In these types of investments, you always have the possibility that upon selling you would get back less than you invested. But it is also possible that these investments will appreciate faster than the rate of inflation.

Finally, the top of the pyramid includes investments such as limited partnerships or collectibles. These types of investments involve more risk because they generally cannot be sold as readily as stocks and bonds and the commissions and costs of doing business are often much higher.

Risk levels in all of these broad categories can be broken down into subgroups. Real estate investments, for example, include rental property, shares of an equity real estate investment trust, a mortgage real estate investment trust, an all-cash real estate limited partnership and a highly leveraged real estate limited partnership. Each type of investment fits someplace on the risk investment profile. When you understand your own risk tolerance, you can eliminate many types of investments that don't conform to your standards.

What do you want from your investments? Will they provide you with safety, growth or appreciation, income or tax savings? No single investment can provide all of these qualities. A balanced portfolio is developed when you prioritize your needs. With careful attention, you can eliminate many investment vehicles that do not contribute to your overall plan. The distribution of balancing factors varies according to each investor, as you'll see in the three case studies that follow.

Doris L., a retired nurse, wanted investments that were completely safe and would not risk her principal in any way. When she found that she was limited to a very narrow field of investments that paid low interest rates, she realized she wanted a high income, too. Because she had recently retired and looked forward to many work-free years ahead, she decided some money should be invested in areas that would provide growth. She resolved this dilemma by investing 60 percent of her money in investments that would not risk her principal, 30 percent in income-producing investments, and the remaining 10 percent in growth-oriented investments, where she would benefit from the appreciation.

Janie C., by contrast, was in her late forties and was fully employed but looking ahead. Her goal was to retire comfortably at age 62. She put 40 percent of her savings into debt investments (for example, Certificates of Deposit) that served to protect her principal, and 60 percent into equity investments such as real estate and high-quality blue-chip stocks. Her primary objective was growth.

Susan K. was just starting out in the work force. She understood the risk and realized that the stocks and mutual funds she purchased were for the long term. She invested in a mutual fund on a monthly basis and was able to average the cost of the share price throughout good and bad markets, a concept known as dollar-cost averaging. She kept a cash fund as insurance against emergencies. The bulk of her investment dollars were higher on the pyramid in the equity market.

A great deal of money is not necessary before you begin investing. Many mutual funds can be opened with an initial investment of $100 and require subsequent investments of only $25. If you had only $500 to work with, you could still have a diversified portfolio that might include $150 in a bank savings account, $200 in a blue-chip stock mutual fund, and $150 in a real estate investment trust. You are ready to invest with peace of mind when all possible contingencies are covered either through insurance or an emergency fund. It's important to take the leap and begin.

Three customary guidelines to follow when investing funds are proper selection, diversification, and constant supervision.

Selection
Most people choose a particular investment because it sounds good to them, rather than setting goals first and then choosing an investment that achieves those goals. The benefits of investments include growth

or appreciation, income, tax-savings, and safety. No one investment can provide all of these benefits equally. Your portfolio might include some investments designed primarily for income and others designed primarily for growth.

John V. was retired and a conservative investor. His primary investment objective was safety and a secondary objective was income. Consequently, he invested his money in certificates of deposit and Treasury Bills. With these investments, his principal was protected and he lived off the interest. One day he attended a seminar promoting an oil and gas drilling program. He was swept away with the promises and enthusiasm of the promoter. He made a substantial investment without regard to his investment goals and objectives and subsequently lost a great deal of money.

John's story reminds us not to be led astray by what neighbors or friends are doing. They might regard risk in an entirely different manner than you do, or there may be particular circumstances that apply to them that don't apply to you. Whenever you consider any new investment, the first question should be, "Is it right for ME?" Ask these questions before you invest:

1. Does the investment objective meet your financial objective? If this offer is a terrific growth investment but you want income next year, then the investment is not appropriate for you. Don't get carried away with the sales pitch. Think first about what you want, then find an investment that fits.

2. What will be your estimated "total return"? Return can come in two forms: income and growth. Some investments offer only one or the other. Investing in gold or silver coins, for example, provides no income, only a growth potential. Some ads in the paper describe total return that people often interpret as interest. Make sure you understand the terms.

3. Is the projected return realistic? No one can see into the future. If you are told the investment "can't lose," move on to the next one. Many people believe you can't lose on California real estate, but some San Francisco homeowners can't find buyers.

4. What is the track record of the managers involved? A good track record is not a guarantee of future performance but can be an indication that the managers have weathered some storms. Find out as much as you can about the people in charge.

5. What are the costs involved? There are always costs of doing business. Make sure all commissions and fees have been explained in detail to you.

6. What are the tax consequences of the investment? The taxes on an investment can have a significant impact. Know in advance the tax consequences of any financial decision.

7. Know how to get out before you get in. Make sure you completely understand the procedure and the costs involved with getting out of the investment.

8. Consider how the investment is being marketed to you. Make sure the person is reliable and has a commitment to remaining in the area.

9. Is the potential return worth the risk? There is risk in every type of investment, and the return is usually in line with the risk. The old adage still holds: If it sounds too good to be true, it probably is.

10. Will this investment add to your diversification? No one investment remains in favor permanently. Make sure your finances are spread among fixed and guaranteed investments, stocks, bonds, and real estate.

Diversification
Safety in investments comes from adequate diversification. This is a basic financial principle, although it is often ignored.

Jane B. needed to supplement her small retirement income. She heard about a company that invested in second trust deeds and promised to pay 17 percent interest. She invested $10,000, much of her life savings, in a second trust deed. The interest came in regularly each month for awhile. Then, without explanation, the interest checks stopped. She received a letter requesting an additional investment so that the situation could be addressed legally. Still no interest checks arrived. Yet another letter ar-

Susan and her husband, both in their 40s, had no children and had saved carefully for the down-payment on a house. Barbara, who was the same age, was divorced and had a teen-age daughter living at home. She had sold her condo for a slight profit and moved up into a single-family home.

Each bought a house about the same time. Susan was enthusiastic about the advantages of a fifteen-year mortgage. "Just think, we'll own our house clear in just a few years."

Barbara nodded. "That's great, but in my case, I only have one income, and the payments on a short-term mortgage are too high for me. I'm taking the 30-year loan, but I plan to pay an extra $100 a month on the principal."

Two years later, Susan's husband was disabled, and their house payments were an excessive burden. They missed payments and had to refinance under conditions that were expensive.

Barbara had a temporary financial setback, due to an emergency appendectomy her daughter had to have. She was not able to make her extra payment for while. In a few months, she was able to resume making the extra payments. Her credit rating with the mortgage company was not affected. Susan's account showed late charges and payment difficulties.

rived requesting more funds. In the end, Jane invested a total of $15,000 into the second trust deed, received little income from the investment, and lost much of her life savings. Diversifying your investments can help you avoid a devastating loss.

Constant Supervision

Watch your investments to make sure they are performing according to your expectations. Decide when you will sell even before you purchase mutual funds or individual stocks. People spend sleepless nights trying to decide whether or not they should hold onto a mutual fund or stock when it starts to go down in value. If, before you purchase the stock, you decide to sell it if it ever goes 15 percent lower, the decision can be made without agony. You will be out the money, but at least you faced this possibility when you made the investment initially.

As you prepare to make investments, you can do so alone or you can work with a financial planner, stockbroker, banker, or other financial adviser. Think about the type of client you are and the type of service you want. Describe your situation to see if it matches the planner's client profile. Some planners work only with people who have a specified income and net worth. Other planners enjoy working with people who have little or no savings but want to begin an investment program with $25 or $50 a month. Call several firms to ask about their fee structure and client base. Questions you might ask include:

- Who is your typical client?
- What is the minimum amount you will handle?
- How are you compensated?
- How long have you been in the field?
- Do you represent a particular type of investment?
- How did you get started?

Anyone can call himself or herself a financial planner, so do not hesitate to ask questions regarding the planner's credentials. Check the planner's educational background as well as the length of time he or she has been in the financial business. Although not a guarantee of excellence, the certified financial planner designation indicates some effort, competence, and commitment on the part of the adviser. Look for some combination of technical and personal skills. Someone with an MBA may not be able to communicate with you on the level you need. It's best to work with someone who has experience and who is current with professional literature, but at the same time, your adviser should address your needs sympathetically.

Easy Action List

- Ask friends for references.
- Interview three financial planners.

Unfortunately, women sometimes feel intimidated and inept when dealing with financial issues. Sally S. had long allowed her husband to make all financial decisions for the family. When her husband died, she allowed the family's financial adviser to make these decisions. But she became increasingly uncomfortable with this situation and began taking classes in financial planning at the local community college. She asked more questions and began to take a more active role in decision-making, much to the displeasure of the family adviser. She noticed his increasing unwillingness to answer her questions, and she finally decided to change planners, but not before telling the adviser the reasons for her change.

Unfortunately, some financial planners exploit this feeling of passivity and pressure clients to follow recommendations blindly. Before speaking to any financial planner, clarify your goals. Recognize that the financial adviser is working for you. It is the adviser's professional responsibility to work from your vantage point in a respectful manner. If you sense the planner is being condescending or intimidating, find another. You are paying for services and deserve to be treated well.

Make sure that all fees and charges are fully disclosed in advance. Some planners make money only from client's fees, whereas others make commissions on products they represent and sell. Some people prefer to work with fee-only planners to be assured of objectivity with investment recommendations, but that fee-only planner might be tempted to give you a lot of generic, prewritten pages to justify a larger fee. On the other hand, planners who are paid commissions might try to sell you something that is not in your best interest. When all expenses are discussed in advance, you have an opportunity to compare costs as you compare advisers.

Meet with the planner initially to learn about his or her philosophy. Present a hypothetical situation to several planners and compare results to find the one you prefer. If possible, attend seminars or classes given by that person, so that you will have an opportunity to evaluate the planner's capabilities without the pressure of a face-to-face meeting.

Before any investment recommendations are made, the adviser should find out a great deal about you, your current lifestyle, and your goals. You will be sharing all your intimate financial data so that she or he can get a clear picture of your needs. Find someone with whom you feel comfortable emotionally before you divulge this information. If the financial planning process is carried out correctly, this should be a long-term relationship. Trust is essential; do not rely blindly on the planner's judgment. Do your own homework and read on the topic independently so you will be able to ask the questions that are important to you. Your visit to a planner should be a conversation, not a speech by the planner. Make it a habit to consider for a day any recommendations before you make a decision. Advisers are expert at presenting a proposal favorably. You should feel comfortable with the decision both emotionally and intellectually.

If you work with a financial planner or other professional adviser, meet with that adviser on a regular basis. Review your goals and your investments periodically or whenever a lifestyle change occurs. Be in charge of your investments just as you are in charge of other areas of your life. You are the only one who can decide your risk comfort level. Manage your investments and your risk level in a manner that is comfortable for you.

Easy Action List

- Invest a small amount of money in a new investment.
- Read financial pages of newspapers.
- Read select magazines.
- Read other key books on investing.

Planning Chart—Chapter 8

Your age now:

20s	30s	40s	50s
Begin program of education for saving and investing	Attend classes and read books	Same	Same
Establish risk levels and patterns	Adjust according to goals and age	Same	Same
	Become established with advisers, financial and tax	Evaluate	Same
	Evaluate investments	Same	Same

Myth-Information

—Evaluating Investment Opportunities

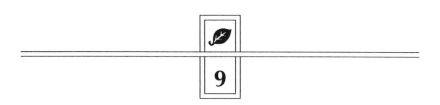

Financial independence in retirement is the primary goal of many people. Yet when they fail to meet that goal, they do so without understanding the reason. Perhaps they succumbed to myths that are popularly regarded as fact. In this chapter we will examine some of those myths. Here is an example to start.

Myth: *You can always make money in real estate.*

Fact: *While it is true that real estate is a viable investment, particularly in certain sections of the nation, making a profit in real estate involves many factors.*

Timing and location remain major ingredients in the real estate success story. If a company requires a worker to move, perhaps because of a transfer brought on by a factory closing, that worker has little control of timing and location in either selling or buying a home.

Some real estate investments require specific knowledge and skills. Rental properties, for example, need attention when vacant or repairs when occupied. The owner must respond in order to protect her investment. An alternative is to hire professional property managers, but their fees reduce the profit margin.

Real estate, like other investments, should be chosen after careful analysis of all requirements of maintenance and upkeep. In addition, different types of real estate meet different goals. Risk, cash flow, income potential, and other factors should be studied in light of your present and future needs.

Rule Number 1:   Goals Must Be Established Before Investments Are Chosen

Only then will financial choices fit and contribute toward achievement of goals.

Myth: *Prices will never be as low as they are now.*

Fact: *Prices may generally be rising, but good buys, even bargains, are usually available in the marketplace, whether in stocks, real estate, or used cars.*

The secret is to find them, a requirement that includes both patience and diligence. An investment that sounds like a bargain because of low price may not be one if it has a low rate of return or if the company has a poor credit rating.

Rule Number 2:   Beware of the Words 'Never' and 'Always'

They cover more territory than can be imagined.

Myth: *I don't have to save for retirement; I'll inherit enough.*

Fact: *This may seem true at face value, but is it really so?*

One couple, the T.'s, thought so. Mrs. T.'s parents had a large, comfortable home, paid for, and better than average savings. All this, along with her father's pension, allowed them to live an ideal retirement life.

Closer examination of the circumstances revealed that her parents were healthy and energetic at the present time. Given the ages of all the parties, it was quite likely that the T.'s would be facing retirement while her parents were still living. The T.'s should also consider the possibility that either of Mrs. T.'s parents might be stricken with a long-term illness requiring nursing home care, which could deplete much of their estate. In addition, Mrs. T. has to share this estate with a brother and a sister.

**Rule Number 3:   Plan to Be as Independent as Possible—
Too Many Unforeseen Circumstances
Can Interfere**

Myth: My husband will take care of me.

Fact: Most women face retirement alone.

A glance at the divorce statistics shows millions of women who will not have husbands to protect them in their retirement years. Further, the average age at which women are widowed is 56. Married women who are removed from the threat of divorce are never far from the specter of death. Karen B. was happily married. One day, her husband, Ken, complained of a headache. The next day he was dead at age 43 of an aneurysm, a ruptured blood vessel in the brain. She was devastated by the shock, and further impaired by the fact that he had always taken care of their financial decisions. At a time when she was emotionally drained, she had to assume command.

**Rule Number 4:   A Woman Should Be a Full and
Active Partner in the Financial
Matters of a Family**

If her husband feels uncomfortable or even threatened by her interest, she might:

- explain that it makes her a better partner.
- point out that she could handle matters better if he were temporarily disabled.
- study investment opportunities and make recommendations for their joint consideration.

Myth: *I'm young; I've got plenty of time to decide.*

Fact: *The best time to start is now. You will never be younger than you are today.*

Rule Number 5: Today Is the Best Time to Start Planning and Saving

The magic of compounding makes money work twice as hard, especially when the habit of saving begins early. Emergencies do not always wait until late in life to happen. The earlier you start, the smaller the increments you need to set aside. Earnings may be lower at an earlier age, but small amounts regularly deposited add up quickly.

Myth: *Old people are very lonely.*

Fact: *While the popular stereotype of the elderly cites loneliness as a dominant factor, research among the elderly does not support that image.*

The Louis Harris and Associates group conducted two studies, one in 1975, another in 1981. In each instance, the result were the same: 60 percent of the general, all-age sample questioned felt that loneliness was a "very serious" problem for most elderly people, whereas only 12 percent of respondents 65 and older felt it was a very serious problem for them personally.[1]

One researcher, who has worked with widows who complained of loneliness, defined the feeling as:

1. A desire to continue an interaction with someone who is no longer available.
2. A feeling that one is no longer loved.
3. An absence of anyone to care for and be a recipient of love.
4. A longing for a relationship similar to one that has been lost.
5. A longing for another person within the dwelling unit.
6. A lack of anyone to share work with.

7.   A homesickness for a former lifestyle or activity.

8.   An alienation due to a drop in status.

9.   An inability to make new friends, due to a lack of social skills.

10.   A combination of any of the above feelings.[2]

Some of these feelings are based on emotional isolation, while others are related to social relationships. Steps can be taken to correct the emptiness that each factor presents. For instance, you can make a deliberate effort to improve social skills by becoming more tolerant of the ideas of others, by overcoming shyness or self-consciousness, and by learning to enjoy the talents and contributions of other people (who may be suffering from the same feelings of insecurity).

When the loss of a loved one is suffered, the remaining person feels a great void. That emptiness can never be entirely filled because every person has a unique combination of characteristics. It is possible for you to carry the joy of the departed person's life within you and still develop and appreciate new friends. You do not deny or repudiate the one who is gone, you are getting on with your own life.

Widows sometimes sanctify their departed husbands, even to the extent of forgetting that they frequently quarreled or were not especially compatible. Unfortunately, this creates an artificial barrier which bars future relationships—who can live up to a saint? From the viewpoint of someone who would like to become closer, friendship is unachievable.[3]

The more aware you are of a problem and the more conscious you are of your ability to overcome it, the less likely it is to continue. Time is on the side of the younger person who can often replace close relationships satisfactorily; but for older persons it is more difficult to find the same level of happiness in the healing and replacement process. The remedy is to be aware and put in extra effort, knowing that new friendships take time to develop and that each person has unique qualities to offer. Focusing on the special characteristics that make a person different from everyone else in the world will help. In other words, live outwardly instead of inwardly.[4]

Rule Number 6: Work at Developing and Keeping Relationships in Good Order

The cure for that lonely feeling is to have fascinating and exciting projects going on, to have interesting and understanding friends to enjoy, and to keep family relationships steady.

Connie K. has three grown children, all married. She has been divorced for many years. "There are times when I could just clobber my daughter, the way she lets her kids get away with things around the house. But I have learned to keep my big mouth shut, and put on what I call 'The Frozen Smile.' You would be surprised how our relationship improved once I discovered this trick. The same works with both of my daughters-in-law. I often wonder if my mother did the same thing after I was married. I know I must have been a real pain sometimes, but she was always sweet. I really appreciate that in her now."

Easy Action List

- Identify one trait that you have that may annoy others. Do you
    - —interrupt?
    - —talk too much?
    - —insist on having your own way?
    - —become impatient when others are slow?
- Begin to work this week to improve that trait.

Myth: **The Government (aside from Social Security) will take care of me.**

Fact: **Resources are limited, and the competition among social programs, national defense, and public education will continue.**

As the large group of the population born in the decade of the 1950s grows older, resources will be more limited. The inevitable result will be lower standards. The handwriting is on the public wall; you will be expected to accept greater responsibility for the costs of your own retirement.[5] As important as saving is managing the money you save so that it will do the best possible job for you.[6]

Rule Number 7:   You Are the Best Person to
                     Look After You

You have been living with yourself for a long time; who better to know what you want? You deserve to have a secure and happy retirement.

Myth: *My company pension will always be there for me.*

Fact: *Headlines in newspapers frequently tell of the takeovers and mergers that displace workers and rearrange companies.*

Keep an eye on your pension plan. Read the fine print in the labor contract relating to the plan. Ask questions. The administrators of the plan should provide the members with a full accounting. Rule Number 7, above, applies here too.

Myth: *My broker knows best.*

Fact: *Your broker is your agent, and should follow your directions.*

Although he or she may have the technical expertise to place orders to buy or sell, that person is there to serve you. You are the person in command, so take the lead. Establish your goals, then clearly state them to your broker. Over time, your goals will undoubtedly change, as your life will change. Instructions to your broker should mirror those changes. If you are not comfortable with the person representing you, shop around for a new broker. Sometimes you find a person with whom you work very well, but who changes jobs. Your broker may ask you to follow her to the new agency. You may want to transfer your account to keep your relationship going, but if you do not want to do so, you are under no obligation to change. It is your decision.

Rule Number 8:   Make Decisions in Your Best
                     Interests, not Because Someone
                     Else Expects You to Act

Myth: *I'll always live just as I do now.*

Fact: *You may not always want to do that. Further, it may not be in your best interest.*

A large house with a huge yard may become a burden if physical incapacity will not allow you the same level of activity you once had. You may choose to move closer to a friend or family. Your neighborhood may not be as safe as it once was. You may consider moving into a retirement community in the Sunbelt, or sharing your household with another. Shared housing is an attractive alternative to living alone, as millions have seen on the TV program "Golden Girls." The plan is simple—the owner or tenant of large living quarters rents or sublets space and shares with others. You may find this is a good plan for you in your retirement years.

Rule Number 9:   Keep an Open Mind to Change

Change, if carefully thought out, can be beneficial. The answer is to move slowly. The typical victim of con artists is the person who allows greed to overcome reason and who is hurried into foolish decisions. Any proposed change should be considered from every angle, so there will be no, or very few, surprises when the event takes place.

Myth: *I heard about a good stock at lunch, I should buy some before everyone hears about it and drives up the price.*

Fact: *Professionals in the heart of Wall Street have research departments and technical analyses to assist them in their stock selections.*

As discussed in detail in Chapter 8, before you make such an investment, be sure to ask yourself a few questions.

1. Does the investment make sense logically and emotionally? One of the authors had one of those wonderful opportunities to invest, but did not like the arrangement because (a) the return was too good to be true and (b) parts of the deal couldn't be put on paper, only sealed with a handshake. Her question to herself was: What happens if this person drops dead from a heart attack—what good would his handshake do me then? As it happened, he was later convicted of defrauding investors. Ask yourself: Can I live with the terms and conditions being offered?

2. What is the track record of the company to which you are giving your money? Your brokerage house can provide the prospectus on almost any company (the Security and Exchange Commission has strict rules about informing the buyer of the fiscal well-being of a company). This material is available to you at no cost.

3. How do I get out? Just as with the home you own (either you will sell or your heirs will someday), so resale should always be part of your *purchase* consideration. Many people were disappointed with limited partnerships when they found it was difficult and sometimes impossible to get out without a loss.

4. Does this investment fit into my overall plans and objectives? Let your goals be your guidelines. Investigate further before you buy, with the same diligence you would use to find a second opinion before having elective surgery.

Rule Number 12: Caution Is Your Friend

Myths are too easy to believe. Learn to be a professional skeptic, and question the logic behind each one. This is called *looking after YOU*.

Endnotes

1. Louis Harris and Associates. *The Myth and Reality of Aging in America* (Washington, DC: National Council on the Aging, 1975).

   _____. *Aging in the Eighties: America in Transition* (Washington, DC: National Council on the Aging, 1981).

2. Rubinstein, Robert L. *Singular Paths: Old Men Living Alone* (New York: Columbia University Press, 1986), p. 190.

3. Ibid., p. 193.

4. Ibid., p. 197.

5. Vicker, Ray. *The Dow Jones-Irwin Guide to Retirement Planning*, second edition (Homewood, Ill.: Dow Jones-Irwin: 1987), p. 14.

6. Ibid., p. 68.

Planning Chart—Chapter 9

Your age now:

20s	30s	40s	50s
Establish methods of challenging assumptions	Practice assertive-ness, independent thinking	Same	Same

Cultivating Your Investment Options

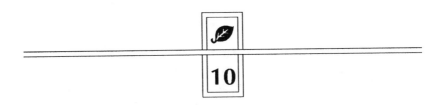

Before making any investment decisions, it is essential to establish goals, have adequate insurance, and have sufficient cash reserves in place. Investments, as described in Chapter 8, can be divided into two main categories: equity, or ownership, dollar investments, and fixed-dollar investments. Although many choices exist, a popular vehicle for investing ownership dollars is mutual funds. People are often intrigued about the stock market but are nervous about putting a large amount of money into one particular stock. A mutual fund is an investment that pools money from many investors with similar objectives. The money, which is placed in many companies in different industries, is professionally managed, which allows investors to invest in the stock and bond markets with the security of knowing a trained person is making the buying and selling decisions.

Mutual funds offer a number of advantages:

- You can make a small initial investment. Although investment requirements differ, some funds require initial investments of only $100, with subsequent investments of $25.

- You can authorize additional investments to be made automatically from your checking account on a regular basis. Additional amounts may be added over the required amount at any time.

- You can reinvest your dividends or have them sent to you, and you can alter that request anytime.

- You can switch your money from one fund in the family to another whenever your objectives change.

- You can withdraw money at any time by following the fund's guidelines.

- You can diversify your money and have it professionally managed.

The major disadvantage to mutual fund investing is the same as with any ownership-dollar investment. If the investment decreases in value, at some point your investment may be worth less than the amount you invested. You can withdraw your money from a mutual fund at any time, but there is no guarantee regarding the amount of your balance. That amount may be more than the amount you invested, the same as the amount you invested, or possibly, less than the amount you invested. This realization makes many investors reluctant to invest, but the advantage of a mutual fund is compelling—the opportunity for your money to grow at a rate that is higher than inflation and taxes.

Rule Number1:   Select the Appropriate Type of Fund

Because people have different goals and objectives, many types of mutual funds are available today. The Investment Company Institute, the trade association for the fund industry, classifies mutual funds into the following categories:

- aggressive growth funds
- growth funds
- growth and income funds
- precious metals funds
- international funds
- balanced funds
- income funds

- option/income funds
- government bonds funds
- GNMA funds (Government National Mortgage Association obligations)
- corporate bond funds
- municipal bonds funds

Most fund companies offer funds in many of these categories, (referred to as a *family* of funds). An investor can change from one kind of fund in a family to another as her lifestyle or philosophy dictates. Information about mutual funds is readily available from financial advisers and from the mutual fund companies themselves. Many funds advertise regularly in magazines and newspapers.

Easy Action List

- Investigate characteristics of fund types.
- Select the appropriate type of fund for you.

Rule Number 2:   Change Investments as Needed

Eileen B. began investing in mutual funds when she was 25 years old. She decided she was in the investment for the long run and was willing to take some chances. She invested $500 in an aggressive growth fund and added $100 a month. At 35, Eileen decided she no longer wanted to be so aggressive with her investment dollars, so she transferred her money into the company's growth fund. When she reaches the next decade in her life, she may decide to transfer the money into a blue-chip or high-grade growth and income fund and then, upon retirement, switch into an income fund that will provide her with monthly or quarterly payments.

Eileen could have invested differently. She could have started a different fund at each decade and allowed the previous fund to compound without making any additional investments. But whatever her choices, she did several important things: she started investing and moved beyond just thinking about it, and she invested a specific amount regularly (which is called Dollar Cost Averaging).

Rule Number 3: Use Dollar Cost Averaging

Eileen was able to purchase more shares when the stock decreased in price and fewer shares at higher price levels. (This procedure will move the average cost per share below the average of the prices at which the shares are purchased. People are more inclined to invest when the market is high and stop investing as the market declines.) Eileen was wise enough to follow this procedure consistently and effectively lowered her break-even point. Here is an example of dollar cost averaging in *down*, *up*, and variable markets:

Down Market

Price Per Share	Amount Invested	Shares Purchased
$ 25	$100	4.0
20	100	5.0
15	100	6.7
10	100	10.0
5	100	20.0
$ 75	$500	45.7

Average Price Per Share: $75 ÷ 5 deposits = $15.00
Average Cost Per Share: $500 ÷ 45.7 Shares = $10.94

Up Market

Price Per Share	Amount Invested	Shares Purchased
$ 5	$100	20.0
10	100	10.0
15	100	6.7
20	100	5.0
25	100	4.0
$ 75	$500	45.7

Average Price Per Share: $75 ÷ 5 deposits = $15.00
Average Cost Per Share: $500 ÷ 45.7 Shares = $10.94

Variable Market

Price Per Share	Amount Invested	Shares Purchased
$ 10	$100	10.0
15	100	6.7
10	100	10.0
5	100	20.0
10	100	10.0
$ 50	$500	56.7

Average Price Per Share: $50 ÷ 5 deposits = $10.00
Average Cost Per Share: $500 ÷ 56.7 Shares = $8.82

You can keep track of your average cost by completing the worksheet provided in Exhibit 10-1.

Since hundreds of mutual fund companies exist, it can be difficult to choose the most appropriate fund. If you work with a professional financial planner, she will probably suggest various companies to use. In return for this advice, she will receive compensation through an hourly fee and/or compensation from the fund, called a *load*. This charge is generally included in the purchase price of the fund but is sometimes added at the time of withdrawal. All charges and costs are described in the prospectus that must be given to you before you invest. Your financial planner should review all the charges with you, making sure you understand each item.

You can save the front-end or back-end charges by making your own mutual fund selection. The process requires a great deal of time, education, and energy. Many investors evaluate funds solely on their track records. While the performance history is important and needs to be considered, it should not be the only selection criteria. Instead, both the track record and the portfolio management team must be evaluated.

It is relatively easy to find out how a fund has performed. Many magazines, including *Business Week, Money, Forbes, and Changing*

Exhibit 10–1

Dollar Cost Averaging Worksheet

Date	Price Per Share	Amount Invested	Shares Acquired

Times, publish the annual performance records of mutual funds. Several publications such as *Johnson Charts* and *Standard and Poor's/ Lipper* are published exclusively to report performance.

According to Michael D. Hirsch, author of *Multifund Investing*, it is essential to find mutual funds with track records that are consistently above-average performers for each of the past three, five, or 10 years. Mutual funds should be considered long-term investments, so you want to find a fund that has consistently performed in the top half of all funds in that category in each of those years. The cumulative returns that the funds readily make available do not provide this information. This information is available but is more difficult to find.

Easy Action List

- Purchase two magazines that list fund performance.
- Select three funds in your category.
- Send for the prospectus.

Once you have narrowed the field of choices, you must then begin to examine the portfolio management team. Some of the magazines now provide the name of the portfolio manager and the number of years he or she has worked with the fund. If you find a performance history that you like, but realize that the portfolio manager is new, then the track record cannot be viewed as an indication of the manager's performance. Information about the portfolio manager is important and not as easy to acquire. A good financial planner will visit the portfolio managers of funds she uses regularly and will pass that information along to you. In his book, Hirsch offers a list of questions you might ask the portfolio manager. The difficulty is getting to the right person. The fund's marketing people will try to intervene to answer your questions so the portfolio manager can continue with his or her work. If you are evaluating a 10-year track record and the portfolio manager has been there during those 10 years, you can reasonably conclude, without actually talking to the portfolio manager, that the fund will continue with the same philosophy.

Olivia and her husband retired to grow peaches, a far different life from the one they had led. He had been an engineering professor at an eastern university, and she had taught at the local high school.

Olivia said, "I was really surprised at how difficult retirement and everything it entails is. It's a stepping stone into another part of my life. It's complicated. There are so many decisions to be made. It's a big, big step. This was a surprise to me. I was afraid of making a mistakes in finances, healthcare, and even socially. I was afraid of losing old friends and hesitant about making new ones. It was a bigger step than I had imagined.

"I think the biggest disappointment was losing touch with old friends. I used to be active in the Women's Club at the University, the Women's Network, and a service club. During my last year on the job, I gave those up, and I distanced myself from those women.

"When I retired, I joined senior groups. I was younger than many of the other members. We weren't interested in the same things. There was a lot of in-fighting in the organizations. They were interested in pastimes and themselves. It's so introspective, and they seemed to have lost touch with the outside world.

"AARP is really great. Here are retired people who are looking outward. She paused, looking at the traffic passing the window at her side. *"Pete and I began reading books on retirement before either of us took the step. We read about retirement, financial matters, social adjustments, and psychology, too. There's a saying in my family, 'If Livvy doesn't know how, she'll go to the library and find out.'*

"I listen to radio talk shows. Every problem in the world comes up, especially financial and legal problems. One case I heard was in the financial area. A woman had invested most of her life savings in a limited partnership that was not liquid and not safe. She put in something like $25,000 and now it was valued at $750. I heard a lot about 'churning,' where the adviser keeps

recommending that the investor move from company to company. Of course, with each switch, the adviser gets a commission.

"First comes earning, then comes learning, and last comes enjoying. I was a little late with the learning part. Now, I keep track of what's going on financially. I spend maybe two days a month total, although it's spread out. I subscribe to Money magazine and a newsletter. I read The Wall Street Journal at the bank or library. I heard about the newsletter on the radio, and I sent for a sample copy before I subscribed.

"I don't let a bad investment go on, I change if I am not comfortable. I am getting more conservative all the time, and am into Treasury notes now. That's a far cry from limited partnerships. And the nicest people tell you about those partnerships, too," she laughed and sipped her tea. "It's a good idea to ask what the commission is on those things. They have to answer you."

She poured another cup of tea and stirred it gently. "I am striving to become my own financial planner, but I have to work on it. There's no end to it, you can't say 'Today I am there.' Learn to be your own best adviser because there's nobody who has more interest in you than you.

"Start early and save all you can, especially if you have a double income. Buy the durable things before you retire, when you have more income.

"I think it's a good idea for a woman to learn some new things, like how to handle a hammer. She will have the time and will need the skill. A house always needs little things done, and hiring a contractor is expensive. The cost of materials is comparatively low, but labor is high.

"If you're married, you must be a team. Even so, every woman should have her own bank account and her own credit cards, in her name. She must build a credit rating. She also must get the minimum number of quarters for Social Security, for the Medicare coverage.

"See what I mean? There are so many decisions to be made," she laughed.

For conservative investors in higher tax brackets, a mutual fund consisting of tax-free municipal bonds is a popular choice. If you purchased bonds individually or in a unit investment trust and held them to maturity, the bonds would fall under the category of a fixed-dollar investment. You would be offered a specific and unchanging interest rate for a predetermined number of years. If you purchase tax-free municipal bonds in a mutual fund, you have then moved into the ownership dollars category. The portfolio manager is continuously buying and selling bonds so there is never a point when you know you will receive your principal in full.

Tax-free municipal bonds provide all the advantages of mutual funds with the additional characteristic that all interest is free from federal tax. If you purchase a tax-free bond fund composed of bonds of only the state in which you live, the interest will be free of both state and federal tax. Tax-free funds pay lower interest rates so the appropriateness of this investment choice is determined in large part by your tax bracket. Check with your tax or financial adviser before investing.

Rule Number 4:   Again, Diversify Your Investments

A popular type of fixed-dollar investment is a tax-deferred annuity. These life insurance products survived tax reform as one of the few remaining ways to postpone paying taxes. Although issued by life insurance companies, these investments provide no life insurance coverage, and you do not have to pass any health requirements to purchase them.

Traditionally, people think of annuities as a contract with an insurance company to pay a certain amount monthly until the investor dies. That is called the *pay-out* or *annuitization phase* of the plan. When you invest money into a tax-deferred annuity, you are involved in the accumulation phase. The major advantage of this investment is that the money will grow and compound tax-deferred. You pay taxes only when you start withdrawing the money, which you cannot do without IRS penalty until you are 59-1/2 years old.

A fixed tax-deferred annuity will provide a set interest rate for a specific time frame. The rate offered is competitive and is generally 1 to 1.5

percent higher than certificate of deposit rates with a guaranteed base rate of 4 percent. Both the interest and the principal are guaranteed by the insurance company but are not guaranteed by the U.S. Government. Most companies promise an interest rate for either a one-year or a three-year time frame. At that time, a new rate will be offered. There are no front-end commissions or charges with a tax-deferred annuity, but there are back-end or surrender penalties that typically operate on a sliding scale for eight years. If you withdraw money the first year, you would pay an 8 percent penalty; the second year, a 7 percent penalty, the third year, 6 percent, and so on.

Because of the surrender penalty, look for insurance companies that provide a bail-out option. For example, a company might offer a 8.75 percent interest rate locked in for three years. If interest rates have dropped and the company offers a renewal rate of only 6 percent, you can withdraw your money or "bail out" without any surrender penalty. Some companies offer attractive first-year rates. Unsuspecting investors may then be disappointed when the rate drops substantially, but the surrender penalty makes it costly to move to another insurance company. A contract, in which all the details are explained, is issued by the company. If you have any questions, immediately contact the person who sold you the investment.

Characteristics of a fixed annuity include:

- Guaranteed principal
- Guaranteed interest
- Taxes deferred until withdrawal
- Earliest withdrawal without IRS penalty—age 59-1/2

An investor can combine the tax-advantage characteristics of a tax-deferred annuity with the potential of a higher return with a variable annuity. In this investment a variety of mutual fund options are offered under the insurance company's annuity umbrella. A variable annuity provides an additional attractive feature: if the owner of the annuity dies, the beneficiary will receive either the fund value or the amount invested, whichever is higher. With this investment, there is no potential loss of principal upon the death of the owner. All costs are described in the prospectus that you receive before you invest.

Mutual funds and tax-deferred annuities are only two of many investment vehicles. These provide an opportunity to invest with small amounts of money and diversify your portfolio between fixed-dollar and ownership-dollar investments. You should aim to diversify your money among the three categories of cash, fixed-dollar investments, and ownership-dollar investments. The worksheet in Exhibit 10–2 will help you look realistically at your level of diversification. The percentages in each category will be determined by your age, stability of income, and comfort level with risk.

It is important to make the best use of the assets available to you to improve the quality of your life and the lives of those around you. It is your responsibility to treat yourself well.

Exhibit 10–2

How Diversified Are Your Investments?

Diversification _____%   _____%   _____%

	Cash	**Fixed**	**Owned**
Taxable Income			
Tax-Deferred Income			
Tax-Free Income			

Planning Chart—Chapter 10

Your age now:

20s	30s	40s	50s
Begin investing	Invest regularly	Diversify	Monitor
	Consider tax-free or tax-deferred investments	Invest in tax-free and tax-deferred investments	Same
	Set up percentage allocation	Evaluate	Same

Choices Abound
—Alternative Retirement Lifestyles

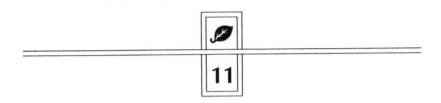

11

As noted in previous chapters, planning is not limited to a set of standards to be achieved only in the far distant future. If you have followed these suggestions and completed some of the worksheets and exercises provided, by now you have a picture of your financial base, and you understand the importance of making plans to achieve the retirement goals you have established.

But your plans, to be effective, must be flexible. Many women are confronted with important lifestyle changes just when they thought things were most stable. After years of marriage, for instance, a woman finds herself alone due to widowhood or divorce—a major change in lifestyle. She might have to struggle to recognize that being alone is not "bad," just different. Learning to live as a single person may cause anxiety for some women. You find obvious advantages in single life. Many women report pleasure in being able to make spur-of-the-moment decisions about travel or eating out; cook only dishes they enjoy; find the towels folded, unless they left them otherwise;

arrange the furniture however they please; and watch what they want on television. Of course, these superficial advantages are only tools to help you through the more difficult parts of being suddenly single. The goal is to make your life's activities your business and appoint yourself the president of your company. Betty B. no longer held a full-time job, but she always announced in a firm voice, "I am *not* retired; I manage my affairs." She used such emphasis that people seldom asked twice.

Rule Number 1:   Consider a Single Lifestyle an Opportunity

Life is full of challenges; when you master problems, you grow and mature.

Easy Action List

- List three things you especially enjoy doing alone.
- Decide on one activity you have always wanted to do.
- Take the first step toward doing it.

Divorce and widowhood are not the happiest options for later years, but growing old with a spouse may also hold some challenging surprises. If a woman has been a homemaker and her husband retires, the amount of time he spends with her increases dramatically.

Sara V. worked with her husband in their construction business. When they sold the business, they both retired—but she soon went to work in an attorney's office. She said, "I've gone back to work to have some freedom. At home, I was the only corporal in the general's army." Each partner should see retirement as a new opportunity.

Easy Action List

- Talk to your spouse about his expectations for retirement.
- Tell him what you see ahead in retirement.

What does retirement mean to you? What do you expect? If a couple completes the exercise below, they will soon find out. Fill out the matrix together, using one subject for each page. Each will identify her or his expectations, and each can see what the other has in mind. Some elements that might be considered are:

- household chores
- getting out of the house/leisure activities
- skills I want to use/develop
- physical exercise
- mental activity/ intellectual pursuits
- contributions to the community, nation, world
- interaction with your children and grandchildren
- style of travel

Expectations of Retirement

Husband's time		Wife's time	
She sees	He sees	She sees	He sees
1. _____	1. _____	1. _____	1. _____
2. _____	2. _____	2. _____	2. _____
3. _____	3. _____	3. _____	3. _____
4. _____	4. _____	4. _____	4. _____
5. _____	5. _____	5. _____	5. _____
6. _____	6. _____	6. _____	6. _____

One of the authors was giving a speech about retirement living. In it she described a single man who had sold everything and spent his time traveling in a motor home, going from one fishing location to another. Because he was single, he was invited to dinner a lot. He commented,

The eight retired women met once a month for lunch to keep alive the friendships they had formed when they all worked at the same company. Each had worked there at least 10 years; one had 23 years' of service. They had gone through all kinds of experiences together—new bosses, reorganizations, severe cutbacks, and innovative programs that did not last long.

Four of them had been typists, one a payroll supervisor, one the cafeteria manager, and two were secretaries. Each considered herself a survivor. The luncheons were especially enjoyable because the women were no longer bound by the clock.

The conversation turned to their level of satisfaction with retirement and advice they would give younger women.

"The day I retired, my life stopped. I had to start all over again," said one. "Someone planning retirement should have a good, really good, hobby."

A second woman said, "It wasn't that way for me. It was like I had never worked at all. I got used to it right away. Retirement was harder on my husband, though. When he was working, he would spend weekends hurrying around trying to get all his extra chores done. After he retired, everyday was Saturday. It took him a while to realize he wasn't going to work Monday morning, so he didn't have to rush to get things done."

"There haven't been any disappointments for me, I just love it," said another. "I miss the association with the people I worked with—that meant a lot to me. That's why I enjoy these luncheons so much," she said with a laugh.

A quiet woman seated at the end of the table said, "I've been disappointed in retirement because my husband's health is so poor that we can't do the things we wanted to do. I guess he waited too long to retire."

"You're right," the first one said. "No one believes he or she will ever be sick or physically unable to get around like they always have."

"I think my biggest problem was I didn't see my work life as a career," another said. "I had to get a job when my husband went back to school for his master's degree, and that's all it was to me, a job. I didn't plan, just went from job to job."

"I said to get a hobby," the first woman said, "but I forgot to mention that you need to get one for your husband, too."

"That reminds me," said another, "If I could tell the world about retirement, I'd ask them to be thoughtful about how they talk to us single folks. We live in such a couple-oriented society, they forget that many of us are alone now, and not by choice. They can say things that hurt without knowing it."

"If I could tell the world about retirement," the quiet one said, "I'd tell them to start saving early. Put something away every month, no matter how small it seems. When you retire, you're suddenly getting along on less."

"I think every married woman should have her own bank account, and she should learn to keep her money in a safe place," the practical one added.

The conversation stopped as dessert was served.

"If I had known how inexpensively I could live, I would have retired years ago." After the speech, a woman came to the front. She was angry. "I've spent years saving so my husband and I could spend our retirement being waited on in luxury and now you've given him this new idea. Shame on you!" That couple needed to talk about their expectations.

Preparation of a comprehensive program for comfort and well-being in your later years is an exciting concept. As you meet your checkpoint goals along the way, apprehension and tension may mount. Your plan becomes a real-life thriller, much like the movie serials of the past—weekly episodes that left the heroine on the brink of some calamity, only to be rescued in the first three minutes of the next chapter.

The only problem with a set scenario is once you get to the point of exercising the plan, circumstances may be different from those originally envisioned.

You may have developed a foundation for comfortable retirement living as you see it now, but part of your planning should address the following possibilities, both personal and financial:

- eroded buying power because of inflation;
- unforeseen crises, such as a lengthy illness of a family member, a natural disaster, or a national economic crisis causing personal financial need;
- unanticipated new interests and activities requiring more funds;
- loss of social contacts or change in identity due to stopping work; or
- need to continue involvement in your local community or the business community, which previously gave you more personal satisfaction than you realized.

These are but a few reasons that may cause you to consider reentry into the work force after formal retirement.

Rule Number 2:   Keep Your Options Open

In 1986, of the approximately 27 million persons age 65 or older in the United States, between 3 and 4 million were in the labor force; most of them were between 65 and 72 years of age, and they worked part-time.[1] Part-time work offers numerous advantages to the older person:

- increased income and feeling of independence,
- active participation in the business community,
- continued sense of identity and belonging,
- increased leisure time over a full-time working schedule,
- opportunities to develop new skills and interests, and
- fewer responsibilities on the job.

A popular plan available through many companies is a partial retirement provision. It provides a reduced work schedule with a phased-in retirement, sometimes with prorated salary and benefits. Many of these plans have a maximum time limit for usage, often five years. This type of plan gives the worker an opportunity to practice retirement. Although it may not have been intended in the original design, it also gives the full-time employee a chance to work part-time to see if she likes that type of employment.

If you change employers between now and retirement, the availability of part-time work for retirees with the new employer may be a factor to investigate as you make the decision to change. Care should be taken when returning to the work force after retirement not to exceed Social Security income limits to prevent penalties (see Chapter 2). Working for your former employer is an attractive choice for you and the company (after all, you are experienced in their routines and you know the staff), but you may wish to consider other options. You may want a flexible work schedule that fits your new lifestyle.

Working through a temporary agency or on a fee-for-service basis is appealing. Employment agencies specializing in temporary help can offer quick work for those with skills and experience or who may be new in a community. Check the phone directory, call an agency, and ask a few questions about the advantages of working there. Some questions you might ask:

- How long have you been in business?
- Are you members of the Chamber of Commerce or Better Business Bureau?
- How many people do you place each month?
- What are the terms and conditions of employment with your agency?
- What benefits do you offer?

You may find yourself ready for a change of pace. The business community rarely remains stationary, and a new occupation could prove more fulfilling than your former line of work. Look for employment more convenient to home, a more pleasant working environment, and higher pay rates. Once you have the stability of a pension, you have greater freedom of choice to find job satisfaction.

Frances K. always wanted to work with animals, but the realities of family life kept her in graphics, the subject she had studied in college. After her retirement, she was able to take a part-time job with the local veterinarian. She was soon taking classes at a nearby university in veterinary medicine. She started a new career, and now works in a field that has been a lifelong interest.

Will you need special skills in your new job? Before you invest time, energy, and money in retraining, survey the job market to be sure jobs are available. A regular review of help-wanted ads in your newspaper will give you an idea of the numbers and kinds of jobs available in your new field.

If you are unsure of what you want to do, you might benefit from researching different occupations, using:

- state employment department career services,
- college or university career and placement offices,
- public library facilities, or

- telephone directory yellow pages listings for "Career and Vocational Counseling."

Retraining and skill development are available from numerous sources. Evening classes are convenient for people who are not able to attend during the day. Community colleges, adult schools connected with high schools, extended education departments from four-year colleges and universities, and countless seminars and workshops are presented by professionals each year. Do not overlook your local public library; it is an invaluable source of information.

Before you finalize your decision, do one last bit of research and consider nontraditional jobs. Often the pay scale will be a pleasant surprise, since nontraditional means a position usually considered a man's job. More and more women are successfully working in nontraditional fields. Since the plans you are considering may take place a number of years ahead, many of these occupations will be more integrated by then, the pioneering phase over. Numerous opportunities are available for women today that were not dreamed of a few years ago, and this trend is expected to continue.

From another perspective, perhaps now is the time to consider a career change. A great deal can be said in favor of the teaching profession, for example. The University of California at Riverside and at Berkeley reports that many of its students in teacher preparation programs have worked in other professions and many are in their 30s and 40s.[2] These people are willing to evaluate career goals and make substantial changes. They know that California will need an estimated 80,000 new teachers before 1992.[3]

Rule Number 3: Don't Make Other People's Decisions for Them

Women sometimes say, "I'm too old" or "They don't want an older worker," and thereby deny themselves opportunities because they assume an employer would not want them. They have made the employer's decision, instead of waiting to find out exactly what that person's choice really is.

Creating Your Own Future

  Pauline had been a school superintendent in the days when a woman's place was in the classroom, not the head office. She always considered herself leadership material, and never settled for anything less. She put in her apprentice years in the classroom teaching math, but kept studying and qualifying for higher and more responsible positions.

"I retired as a school superintendent 17 years ago," Pauline smiled across her living room. "I practiced rocking for a year or two, but rocking is a boring thing to do, so I went into consulting where I started new programs for school districts. I did that for 10 years, and it was wonderful. I got all the fun things to do, yet didn't get stuck with so much of the drudgery. I loved it.

"You have to do something, have some alternatives. I found it was best to build on my background, but in a new direction. You could use a hobby the same way. You might have some hidden wishes or ambitions you never had time to explore."

She leaned forward, her eyes twinkled. "Disappointments? Not a one. I had to change my lifestyle. It went from chaotic to social," she paused to chuckle, "but I found a balance. I find this life very satisfying."

She described her life in a mobile home park, made up exclusively of retired people. "This place is very social, there's as much to do right here as you would ever want." She told how the tenants of the

park banded together to buy the park when the former owners' demands became unreasonable. She was elected to the board of directors of the newly formed corporation, and remains active in the administration of the park.

"I think the biggest surprise was getting used to having so much leisure time. I had been so busy for so many years, I had to learn to pace myself. I was stunned by the fact that there were no demands on my time. We moved to get away from over-organized activities. We wanted a second start, to live where others had no expectations from us."

She said that she was surprised when all her previous professional activities stopped abruptly, and she found the best solution was to find replacement interests.

"At the point of retirement you have to analyze your role in relation to other people. Be aware of your personality assets, review your lifetime accumulation of skills, and figure out what you would like best to do, then do it."

Pauline emphasized the importance of preparing financial budgets, with careful estimates of income and expenditures. She found her plans were fairly accurate.

"We have so many choices nowadays, just remember, you can't go back, so make the present and the future so exciting that you won't even think of it," she laughed and sipped her coffee.

Both federal and state laws forbid discrimination on the basis of age, and with the "graying of America," the median age is going up. Television programs have begun to show older men and women in more attractive roles, much to the delight of audiences. A 1987 television commercial showed a charming scene of an older man leaving home for his first day of work at McDonald's. The vignette sent a powerful message to TV audiences: Older workers are *welcome* at McDonald's. An entire new labor market opened up for the famous fast-food chain, and a new job market became available to older workers. The commercial clearly illustrated an employment condition that was unknown a few years ago. Workers can be ready for new opportunities when they keep their options open. Being flexible about your goals is a goal in itself.

Rule Number 4:   Have a Strategy

A common mistake is to look only at your present job and not consider your career as a whole. As a result, you might stay in the same job too long and let unnoticed opportunities pass by. One way to judge if you have stayed too long is the application of the "Delight Factor."

The dictionary defines delight as a high degree of gratification; extreme satisfaction; something that gives great pleasure; to give keen enjoyment. Do these apply to your present job? If the thrill has diminished, perhaps it is time to shop around. Begin by listing your abilities, skills, special knowledge and talents. Enlist the support of your friends, they may remind you of an overlooked talent or special gift.

Kellie was recently divorced, and was working in the dresses section of a department store. She needed more income, yet had little formal education and, she thought, few marketable skills. In discussing her situation with her friend Wanda, Kellie said that she really liked working with ready-to-wear, and had often been complimented by her friends on her stylish appearance. Wanda said, "Why not be a fashion consultant or personal shopper? You could provide a real service to women who are too busy to shop. Why don't you make a presentation to the head of your department?" They discussed the matter further, and Kellie carefully made her plans. She was frightened when she met with her boss, but the manager saw the advantages to the plan immediately, and, with a few modifications, Kellie was involved in the new service. It gave her a chance to earn more, it brought her to the attention of her boss and other managers, and she had a great deal more job satisfaction.

Kellie had taken her skills for granted, and she undervalued herself and her potential. It took a friend to see a way out. In your plan, start with the ideal. Ask yourself, if I could have any job at all, what would I choose?

Easy Action List

- List three occupations that look interesting.
- Read about one of these this week.

Corinne B. wanted a career change and longed for a position where her income would be directly related to her business savvy. She decided she would like to work in radio sales, but knew little about the field. She made a list of radio stations in her area in order of preference. She worked initially to schedule informational interviews with the station in which she had the *least* interest. Using this technique, she was able to learn a lot about the industry. By the time she was talking to people at her favorite station, she was able to ask thoughtful questions that indicated familiarity with the radio industry. She appeared confident and knowledgeable—traits that would make her stand out when a position opened at the station.

Define what you do *not* want, to help you know what you *do* want. It is easy to separate the conditions that do not appeal to you. You may have a clear idea of what you do not like at all, but what about the middle ground? Would a mediocre job soon become so boring that you would be unhappy? What can you live with? At what point does the delight diminish?

You can use this worksheet to list the aspects that lower your delight factor with your present job:

Creating Your Own Future

Conditions:	N/A	Important	So-So	Not Important
Unpleasant boss				
Unpleasant coworkers				
Low pay				
Long hours				
No recognition of efforts				
Ugly office				
Too noisy				

Add other variables that make a difference to you. What would it take to change the items in the "important" column? Leaving the organization? Transferring to another department or division?

On the second worksheet, list your reasons to stay:

	N/A	Important	So-So	Not Important
I'd have to compete elsewhere				
I'd lose benefits				
I'd lose my pension				
I'd have to make new friends				
I'd have to start over				
Other				

Compare the two worksheets. How do they look? Are there compelling reasons to stay or to go? If you are still unsure, try this sentence stem exercise:

- One of the goals I have is. . .
- More than anything else in my career I want. . .
- One standard of success for me is. . .
- In five years I want to be. . .

When you begin to plot out your career path, many new ideas will come to mind.

New opportunities come to women when they are well *positioned* in the job market. Major companies work hard to have the best market position. A career woman should use the same strategies. When retirement comes, you will have a stronger foundation by virtue of years of exercising your strategy muscles.

Martha T. carefully studied her abilities and skills, and then made a list of the public agencies where she most wanted to work. She evaluated the benefits and the burdens of each organization. She asked questions of employees and read all she could about each organization. Finally she chose the ideal place—the one agency where she knew she would be happy and where she would be most effective. The problem was they had no job openings and had no idea when one would be available. Undaunted, she asked if she could volunteer three afternoons a week. Once they had recovered from the surprise and shock of her offer (no one had ever done *that* before), they accepted. She worked for a few months on that basis. Unexpectedly, a position became available, and she got the job. The agency officials knew her work well by then, and they were impressed with her dedication to their profession. She was fortunate because she could afford to volunteer, and it paid off handsomely for her in the long run.

The best strategy is to place yourself in the optimal position to enhance your career. Everything you do to improve your career status will pay double dividends: immediately and after retirement. Consider the following strategies to improve your position.

Be visible.
Many women have difficulty with this, because they were taught to be passive, and they consider it to be bragging or showing off. In the reality of today's competitive business world, it is essential to make one's talents, skills, and knowledge known. The key to success with this strategy is to do it in an assertive, but not an offensive, manner.

Visibility does not mean being seen in the halls and in the company cafeteria, but associating with the people who have the greatest influence on your work. It also does not mean that you must abandon friends you have made on the job. If they are real friends, and not associations that are required because you work in the same proximity each day, you will have a strong foundation for the friendship.

Talk with those who have direct influence over your position. The Old Boys' Network has worked this way for years. Business luncheons and golf games have been the sites of many decisions. Deal yourself in. At meetings, conferences, workshops, speak to those who influence your professional life. It need not be a prolonged conversation, in fact, a brief greeting may be enough. The idea is they know you are there, and you know that they know.

Impress the boss.

Do you have a proposal or idea for the betterment of your organization? No? Prepare one. Give extra time to answering some of the problems about which you and your boss are concerned. Do your homework; ask yourself the questions the boss would ask. Prepare realistic answers for the most difficult questions that could be asked about your proposal. Arrange to meet with the boss, saying that you have an idea you want to present. Make sure your idea is on paper, with all supporting data, so you can give him or her a written copy to review later.

Just in case you get the cold, steely eye and a dismissal in final tones, have another item or two on your agenda. You will gain the image of being an employee who is thinking about the well-being of the organization. Every employee has an obligation to make the boss look good; managers are very aware of this doctrine.

Easy Action List

- List one problem you could solve at work.
- Prepare in your mind to present your entire solution.
- Read one new professional journal or publication this week.

Join professional organizations.

This action illustrates your commitment and gives you chances to improve your skills. It is an opportunity to make contacts that may come in handy later should you decide to change jobs.

If possible, be a presenter. You may have pertinent information, knowledge, or skills worthy of sharing. Ask to give a workshop at the next conference. If you do not have anything new to share, volunteer to be on the committee developing the conference, or ask if you can introduce a presenter. This is called being visible.

If the idea of speaking in front of others terrifies you, take a class in public speaking at night school.

Easy Action List

- List two professional organizations you could join or ones you now belong to, in which you could be more active.
- Identify a work subject or technique about which you could develop a speech or presentation.
- Take a public speaking class or join Toastmasters.

Learn your way around town.
Town means your business world and its adjuncts. Are the movers and shakers of your world active in politics? Get involved in campaign activities, not only for specific candidates, but for ballot measures that appear at every election, such as school bonds or mass transit measures. Do the workers of your company have sports teams? Although you may hate outdoor games, volunteer to be the hot-dog chef or the team bookkeeper. It will earn you a place in the action, an image, an identity within this circle.

If you take your career seriously, make sure you show it.
Much has been said about nonverbal communication in recent years; more than half of all messages we receive are nonverbal.

Personal appearance is an important way of signaling your dedication to the job. If you constantly dress as though you are on your way to a vacation resort, no one will take you seriously. Your appearance says play instead of work. This was the case with Lisa R., who had two wardrobes, one chic and expensive, the other casual and inexpensive. Unfortunately, she wore the sports clothes to the office, where she was a manager. No one took her seriously, and she diminished both her credibility and effectiveness. The way you choose to decorate your work space will tell volumes. Do you display achievements through awards and trophies? Are your paintings or sculpture in evidence? In every organization, there is always one woman with dozens of African violet plants around her desk, but she is seldom a great influence or power player (unless she owns a company that sells African violets). The plants send the nonverbal message that she is more interested in gardening than in her job.

Study the values your organization emphasizes. Do not guess; look carefully for the signals. If achievement is stressed, pull out the charts and graphs and put away the needlepoint pillows. If teamwork is stressed, display your trophies, framed photos of the team you managed, or the award you got for coordinating the annual blood drive.

Collect letters of reference as you go.
If your boss will retire soon or move on, ask for a letter of reference for your files, so you won't have to bother him or her years later.

If possible, keep originals of all awards and letters of commendation that go into your personnel file. If you have done something special in the community, and the leaders are anxious to show their gratitude, ask them to write a letter to your boss, with a copy to you. Keep these items. You can get ten years of use out of a good letter. People soon forget how wonderful you have been, they move away and you don't know how to reach them, or they die. If you have not asked for a letter, it may be too late to do so at a time when it might help you advance your career.

Rule Number 5:   Know Your Target

Where do you want to go? You need not have a specific position in mind, but you should be able to define the field.

If you are planning to make an occupational change, list the skills you have for that new occupation. For example, let us say that currently you are a secretary in a small wholesale grocery company with no place to advance, and you want to get out of the clerical ranks and into management. Start by making a list of industries that are related and where you could use the knowledge you have acquired in your present job. Look for larger companies in your field, such as restaurant chains, hotel chains (they combine food plus many other jobs), grocery chains, hospitals.

Fill in the grid on this worksheet:

Name of Industry	Women in Management?	Good Pay	Benefits	Plus	Minus
Company A	yes	yes	no	good opp.	move to Alaska
Company B	yes	no	no	no move	

Research is needed to find out the pluses and minuses in working for Company B—perhaps convenience, pleasant atmosphere, or congenial workers would make a difference in favor of this employer. You do not need to whittle it down to only one field; keep two or three main fields in mind, the ones that offer the best opportunities. The plus or minus columns may represent such things as retraining, job hazards, or seasonal work.

How should you decide if a field is attractive? Do not depend on the movies or what you assume may be the facts, but become a job detective. Check the want ads in the big city newspapers' Sunday editions, which are available in the periodicals section of your local library. While you are there, check out professional publications for that industry. In this era of specialization, hundreds of magazines are printed each month for targeted audiences. Your librarian can obtain copies of trade publications for you. Read them carefully and know what is going on in that industry. Is it financially depressed and retrenching, or are they using creative ways to attract new employees?

Rule Number 6:   Your Chances of Reaching Your Goals Are Related to Your Willingness to Take Risks

Risks here doesn't mean anything foolhardy. Do not quit a present job without a better one securely in hand. But do ask yourself: What am

I willing to risk/do/change to achieve my goal? What is your spouse willing to do to help you? If you were to hurry home, breathless and excited, to announce, "Honey, I just got my dream job! We are moving to Boston!" what would his reaction be? Generally, women tend to stay within a 35-mile radius of home when job searching. Ask yourself if you are willing to make a bigger move.

Sally R., a personnel director with a small surgical instrument manufacturer in Arizona, was offered an attractive promotion and substantial raise when her company was bought out. It meant moving to Philadelphia in January. Without hesitation, she accepted. "The offer was so good, I couldn't believe it. I love to ski and I'll learn to adjust to the rest," she said. She was willing to take the risk and to make the changes necessary to reach her goal of advancement. She did not limit herself by turning away from the risk and new opportunities.

Finish the following sentences to help discover how much risk you are willing to take:

- My greatest responsibility in retirement will be. . .
- My greatest freedom in retirement will be. . .
- The greatest change in my lifestyle will be. . .
- The greatest benefit to me as a person will be. . .
- The greatest change in my relationships will be. . .
- The greatest opportunity to me will be. . .

The essence of our advice in this chapter: Don't limit yourself. Give yourself permission to explore new fields. Say, "I'll consider it," not "I can't."

Endnotes

1. Pifer ,Alan, and Bronte, Lydia, eds. *Our Aging Society: Paradox and Promise* (New York: W.W. Norton & Co. 1986), p. 343.

2. Brown, Patricia R. and Koppich, Julia. *Exploring the Link Between Teacher Recruitment and Retention and a Teacher Information System* (San Francisco: Far West Laboratory, 1988), p. 30.

3. Guthrie, James W., and Kirst, Michael W., eds. *Conditions of Education in California 1986-87* (Berkeley, Calif.: Policy Analysis for California Education [PACE], October 1986).

Planning Chart—Chapter 11

Your age now:

20s	30s	40s	50s
Be aware of your likes and dislikes as you find your niche	Observe and evaluate different lifestyles	Discard excesses, learn to say no	Prepare and plan for transition into retirement
Establish first home	Improve home	Same	Evaluate and consider alternate housing
Begin career	Climb in profession	Evaluate and consider change	Fruition and preparation for retirement

Adversity or Opportunity
—Survival Techniques

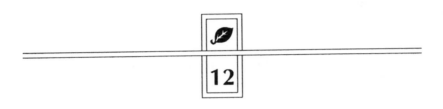

12

Reality may bring rude surprises to those who believe in the popular notion of living happily ever after. Conditions change, and not always for the better. Personal tragedies, such as death of a loved one; public calamities, such as natural disasters, or economic downturns—both can produce unexpected changes and require critical decisions. In addition, loneliness, stress, or depression can internally undermine the quality of life.

Many of these will probably never affect you, but one or two may touch your life. You will be better prepared to cope and overcome these obstacles if you understand what is happening to you, what some of your feelings are likely to be, and how to minimize the effects.

Rule Number 1:   Develop a Stubborn Streak

You may say, "Well, that's easy, I already have one," but now you should learn to put it to use as a survival skill. When adversity strikes, exercise stubbornness by not giving up. Even if you have no idea of how the problem will be resolved, you must be certain, deeply and securely in your own self, that you will find a solution.

See yourself as a survivor—somehow, some way. Each crisis you survive will make you tougher, more resourceful, and better able to face the next problem. A survivor copes with stress. All living activities can create stress, but you can take steps to control inner reactions. Stress produces abnormal reactions to normal situations. Sociologist Jessie Bernard notes that marriage is stress-reducing for men and stress-producing for women.[1]

Easy Action List

- Identify three situations in your life where you faced adversity and survived.
- Imagine yourself in a negative situation, then see yourself resolving the problem.

Stress causes tension, which, in turn, causes the first step of adaptation to begin. Tension is tolerated at different levels by different people. The human system diligently adjusts to the stress levels it encounters, with the goal of reaching manageable limits. Tension is not bad; in fact, certain levels are beneficial and support healthy functioning. Tension and stress in tolerable amounts are important factors in emotional well-being. It is when limits are exceeded that trouble begins. Excessive stress is related to coronary heart disease, hypertension, stroke, disturbances of heart rhythm, migraine headache, and other disorders.[2]

One way to control higher than normal levels of stress is to establish goals that specifically determine your direction. By focusing attention on the goal, you can maximize the use of your energy and minimize immediate tension.[3]

Rule Number 2:   Practice Survival Strategies, Beginning Now

The survivor will examine the causes of the problem and seek ways to learn from the experience. Despite an initial inclination to retreat from adversity, the survivor builds strength by successfully getting through the negative experience.

Dr. Lawrence Al Siebert, psychologist of Portland, Oregon, has studied survivor personalities. He notes that, more than anything else, flexibility and adaptability are key factors to the survivor.[4] The flexible person is one who is able to move from one environment or set of conditions to another, perhaps on very short notice, with a minimum of stress reaction. It is being able to roll with the punches. The adaptability factor comes into play when a person begins in the new environment. The length of time and the ease with which an individual can put new conditions to work for her benefit or protection indicates her adaptability.

The survivor exhibits flexibility by being able to give up old external objects and ideas when necessary, because she knows she can adapt through the application of her inner faith, her sense of humor, and her creativity. Practice flexibility in everyday routines.

Easy Action List

- Identify one daily routine and vary it.
- Notice your feelings when you start a new routine.

Giving up fixed ideas in favor of new, creative notions is an important characteristic of the survivor. Brainstorming, a successful technique often used in business and research, calls for quick exposition of answers to a given problem, with no editorial or judgmental comments by any of the participants. It is also one facet of survival thinking, because it helps a person to be creative. You can practice this skill in many everyday situations, ranging from "Where shall we build the doghouse?" to how to increase the family's income. Do it, and become comfortable doing it. You will then feel at ease when you consider a nontraditional solution to a vital question.

If you are in the habit of thinking in creative ways, you will do it automatically, and because you have had practice, you will do it well.

Rule Number 3:   Keep Your Sense of Humor

Much of the rich supply of American humor has risen from adversity. The tall tales of Pecos Bill and Paul Bunyan were an outlet for people who lived far from luxurious or safe lives. The Great Depression brought forth such laugh provokers as Will Rogers and the Marx Brothers. Laughter eases tension, reduces stress, and restores the equilibrium. Clear thinking is easier after a chuckle and problem-solving more likely.

Rule Number 4:   Ask for What You Want

An estimated 70 percent of those who are entitled to Supplemental Security Income (SSI) under the administration of the Social Security system, do not apply for that benefit. Eligibility, as discussed in Chapter 2, is stringent, so persons who are in need and entitled still must ask.

Asking questions also gives you more information that you can use to make intelligent decisions. If you are planning for certain medical benefits after retirement and are not absolutely sure they will be available to you, ask your carrier's representative, or write to the administrator of the policy for information. If the coverage you desire will not be available to you later at retirement, ask what they do offer. If they reply, "We offer nothing in this line," then ask them to refer you to companies that do offer these specific benefits. Businesspersons always know what their competition is offering, and if they get enough requests, they often will begin to offer the product or service themselves. Keep asking.

Sometimes it it difficult to find the straightforward answers you need. In the example above, the rapidly changing health insurance field and the likelihood of congressional intervention may make your choices less clear. These variables remain speculative, but you must make decisions based on the best information available at any given time. When planning for health benefits some years in advance of actual retirement, you can see the advantage of being well informed. The news media are aware of public interest in these issues and give such matters ample publicity. Be alert to your present and anticipated needs.

Asking for assistance in a personal context may cause you to hesitate, but in today's complex world no one can have all the answers all the time. Requesting answers or special assistance does not mean that you give up your right to make a decision. Keep in mind that everyone needs assistance once in a while. If you feel uncomfortable about asking, it is probably because you are not used to doing it.

A simple way to overcome that uneasiness and feeling of vulnerability is to start small. By using the salami system (one thin slice at a time), you will become comfortable about asking others for occasional support.

Easy Action List

- Read one book or article about becoming assertive.
- Discuss with a friend or someone you admire how they cope with adversity.

Consider the other side of the picture: You enjoy helping others once in a while. Return the favor. It is flattering to other people, especially those who care for you a great deal, when you ask them to do something special for you. Notice that you really make others happy when you allow them to do things to please you. Be careful not to overdo it. Too much salami makes a boring diet.

One way to examine what you are asking for in a personal relationship is to complete the blanks in the following sentence: Because____is happening, I feel _____, and I want_____ (to happen). You might complete it this way: Because layoffs are happening at work, I feel threatened and I want to feel more secure at home. Or perhaps: Because I am upset over the illness of my mother, I feel sad, and I want to help in a positive way so we may both feel better about her condition. This formula can make you aware of your feelings and help you arrange your thoughts in a logical progression, which is important as a survival technique.

Requesting what you want also calls for a specific step on your part. You must know what is wrong, and what to ask for to make things right, or at least better. A statement that something is wrong is not asking for anything. Examine the situation, determine the solution, then frame the question to include the solution or the opportunity to find the solution together.

Rule Number 5: Avoid the "Poor Me" Trap

Adversity, especially in such situations as the death of a loved one, brings an outpouring of sympathy from those nearby, as well it should. While working through the stages of grief, it is easy to fall into the "poor me" trap. All things must change, but some changes come more suddenly or sooner than anyone would have wished. As surely as there is change, there is continuity—life goes on. If you know a newly widowed woman, some of these suggestions may help her.

When a woman is widowed, one of the first realizations she must have is that she didn't die, too. Think of it a moment. When a woman marries, she pledges her future to that of her spouse. A dying person has no future, at least as we know it here on earth. When her husband dies, she may perceive that her future has died, too.

One of the most important and most difficult steps for a widow to take is to recognize that she still has a future. She should begin to ask herself, "What am I going to do with the rest of my life?" a question that acknowledges that she still has a future. True, it may not be as comfortable, and she may have many personal and social adjustments to make, but the future is still in front of her.

For many widows, their first Christmas or holiday season without their husbands is very painful. Something different from the regular family routine should be planned. If the routine remains exactly the same, everyone will feel the loss more than ever. A change, no matter how slight, will tend to emphasize a new perspective. The brainstorming technique could be used to advantage here in deciding what plan could be different.

For years, one family had met with Mom and Dad on Christmas Day at their home for an exchange of gifts and a large dinner. The first

Christmas after their father's death, they all met at the home of the second daughter. Just before they opened their gifts, the eldest son, Bob, read a brief story he had written about the gifts he had received from his father over the years, both material and spiritual. They proceeded to open gifts as usual. They had honored their Dad, yet recognized the change.

Another widow, Molly R., whose husband had passed away early in the year, confided in a friend, also widowed, "I'm dreading Christmas already." The friend suggested a trip to Colonial Williamsburg for Christmas. They went and both had a grand time.

Rule Number 6:   Give Yourself Permission to Seek Happiness

The emotional stress from adversity can sometimes become overwhelming, and dim life's brighter side. Your sense of humor will come into good use here. Rather than dwelling on the negative, try to develop the habit of saying or thinking something positive every time you say or think something negative. Create a philosophical double-entry bookkeeping system: for every debit there must be a credit. It will help you maintain a balance, even when the going gets rough.

Self-reliance is a characteristic of the survivor. You can develop it like a muscle—with use, it grows stronger.

Easy Action List

- Make a list of some advantages of being alone.
- Practice developing a sense of satisfaction when you are doing your favorite "alone" activities. These might include keeping a journal, listening to music, playing a musical instrument, or meditating.

And while you are at it, reevaluate some of the illusions that were important when you were younger. Not many women would choose to go back and live all those years over again—now that they have learned who they really are. Do you really need to make the bed every

Patricia B. does not own a dress, but has many attractive pantsuits. She gave up style for comfort a long time ago. She was never afraid to tackle a tough job; at least, if she was scared, she never let it show. When her husband died, she accepted widowhood and a new turn of events in her life.

Margaret V. had nursed her husband through several lengthy illnesses before he passed away. The toll was heavy on her health. She had to learn to pace herself for the most efficient use of her physical energy.

The two women came to the same restaurant together every evening. Sometimes they ate alone, but, more often than not, they were joined by friends who stopped by for dinner. The conversation was always lively.

Patricia said, "I've been lucky. I have worked all the time. And I'm not afraid of anybody. That makes a big difference. I always earned more than my husband did, but his Social Security benefit was greater than mine.

"My best work I got through his being a Kiwanis member. Nobody recognized my design abilities until I started making a lot of noise about it. Business organizations are really important because they give you the connections you need. Stand on your own two feet. It's up to you to take care of yourself, no one else will.

Margaret agreed. "I taught school for 23 years—I had a child at 43—yet when I went to retire, I was a few months short of eligibility, and I didn't get a cent. It was a good thing we had a business. I was too dumb to find out what the score was.

"You have to have some reserve, and be as independent as you possibly can. I don't have any Social Security of my own because I was a teacher, and they aren't covered. You have a voice, use it."

Patricia buttered her dinner roll, "It's time for women to refuse to be secretary of anything. They need to speak up. When I retired, I refused to cook anymore. We just went out. Now, I eat at a different restaurant for each of the three meals a day; and I have a network of friends at each place. It's loads of fun and never boring."

Margaret grinned, "I love it, too. After dinner, we go to my house or hers and do the crossword puzzle for the day. You can't imagine how good it feels. After being tied for years to a man who was sick and who couldn't understand why I needed any money, this is just great."

morning? Do you have to have the latest fashions, just because it is the thing to do, because a magazine says you must?

Easy Action List

- Name two ways you now express your independence.
- Identify one person you admire for being independent; select one characteristic of that person and try to incorporate it into your life.

Physical activity can help in hard times, too. Jane S., a single parent, unexpectedly lost her job through no fault of her own. It was a devastating blow. At just about that time, a neighbor cut down a large pine tree and hauled in onto the vacant lot next to Jane's home. She took an axe and chopped the tree as hard as she could for two days. On the third day, she dressed carefully and went out and found another job. The physical activity helped her to think through her plans and face the world again.

Easy Action List

- Determine two ways you physically respond to stress.
- Read one article or book about stress this month.

Many women secretly dread their senior years because of the stereotype of the older person as alone and lonely. The number of those living alone is growing rapidly.[5] The stereotype equates living alone with rejection, and overlooks the fact that the two terms are not synonymous. It is possible to be very lonely in a marriage or family group. In fact, living alone seems to stimulate older people and adds to their longevity. In a study by Dr. Mary G. Kovar, released in 1988, of those aged 70 and older living alone who reported regular meetings with friends and neighbors in 1984, 92.5 percent were still alive two years later, and 89.3 percent were still living on their own.[6]

These people have turned the less attractive aspects of living alone into the comforts and satisfactions they desire. They have learned to cherish their independence. A balanced life of social activities and solitude is the key.

Activities provide an identity, the opportunity for self-expression, and a support system in time of need. A few of these might include:

- church-related functions
- folk dancing (one need not have a partner)
- volunteer work at local schools or hospitals
- functions at senior centers
- political campaigns
- classes (attending or instructing)

The balance of this list, to ensure quiet moments, might include:

- reading
- writing your family's history or your life story
- painting, drawing, or other artistic activities
- gardening

Women who have been trained to value their own worth in terms of how popular they are may interpret being alone as a signal of their not being wanted. These women must learn to value their own individuality and cultivate being their own best friend. A passive response to being alone is not a satisfactory solution. Examples of passive time-killers include excesses in any of the following:

- sleep
- watching TV
- drug or alcohol consumption
- eating

Plan to give yourself freedom and allow yourself to experience the joy of doing something new. It does not have to be spectacular or expensive, but it should bring personal satisfaction.

If you have an established daily routine, you will have something to look forward to. From that beginning you can expand outward, learn new skills, and enjoy talents you never realized you had.

Creating Your Own Future

Everyone recognizes change as inevitable, but few realize that some changes will happen slowly, unnoticed over the years. Some changes will take place because your role in the family is different. Children grow up and start their own families, so your role changes from mother-as-decision-maker to grandmother and mother-friend. You should think about the roles that give you great satisfaction but may change. When you are aware of the natural changes that will take place, you will be better prepared to extend them effectively or find parallel outlets. Change means that you must let go of a part of your life. When you do, find a new challenge.

If your new lifestyle decisions do not work as well as you expected, they can be changed. The beauty of accepting a flexible outlook is you can make improvements.

A healthy lifestyle includes giving yourself an occasional treat. Let the emotional sunshine flow in. You will savor every moment. For instance, you might:

- make a phone call to a favorite person
- get a manicure or pedicure
- go to a resort for a weekend
- try a new perfume
- plant a tree
- take a friend or family member on a special trip

Easy Action List

- Make a list of treats, small and large, to be enjoyed at home.
- Have a list of small and large treats you can give others you care for when you feel like it.

Mary H. saved her frequent-flyer bonus points until she had earned a free second ticket. Then she took her 15-year-old grandson to Washington, D.C., for a week. He had studied history and appreciated the significance of the museums and landmarks. The trip was a treat to congratulate him on a special accomplishment in his music. They both had a wonderful time and talked about it for years afterward.

Give up, or better yet don't begin, thinking in extremes. Examples of this type of self-destructive behavior include:

- avoiding in-between compromises, seeing things in all or nothing terms;
- overgeneralizing, seeing things in terms of always or never;
- using the negative approach more than the positive;
- relying on emotional thinking instead of applying logic;
- categorizing and stereotyping people and things; and
- taking the blame for everything, becoming a professional victim.[7]

The balance you will achieve from practicing these rules will bring you the flexibility, serenity, and toughness that will support you and those near you in troubled times.

Endnotes

1. Kinzer, Nora S. *Stress and the American Woman* (Garden City, N.Y.: Anchor Press/Doubleday, 1979), p. 108.

2. Anderson, Robert A., M.D. *Stress Power! How to Turn Tension into Energy* (New York: Human Sciences Press 1978), p. 31.

3. Lura, Alexander R. *The Working Brain* (New York: Basic Books, 1973), p. 57.

4. Siebert, Dr. Lawrence Al. "The Human of the Future: The Synergistic Personality." Paper presented at the Western Psychology Association Convention, San Jose, California, 1985.

5. Powell, Barbara, Ph.D. *Alone, Alive and Well: How to Fight Loneliness and Win* (Emmaus, Pa.: Rodale Press, 1985), p. 15.

6. "Elderly Live Longer When Active, Single." *San Luis Obispo County Telegram-Tribune*, April 16, 1988.

7. Powell, op. cit., p. 57.

Planning Chart—Chapter 12

Your age now:

20s	30s	40s	50s
Collect materials on care of parents	Open discussion with parents and siblings	Set plans in place	Implement plans
	Become aware of resources	Same	Same
Keep life in balance, set priorities	Update and evaluate	Same	Same
Develop survivor skills	Expand same	Same	Same
Develop stress-reducing activities	Adjust as life changes	Same	Same

A Helping Hand
—Resources You Should Know About

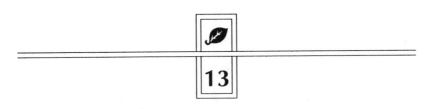

Some of the subjects mentioned in this book may leave you with feelings of anxiety about the future. The lengthy illness of a spouse or parent or inflation eroding your savings are serious matters and cause for concern. Be assured that many resources are, and will be, available to help you handle these problems. The key to dealing with these serious problems is to learn now to rely on resources for everyday issues. If you have practiced using this activity under normal conditions, you are likely to do the same successfully in times of stress.

A wealth of information awaits you at your local library. If you are studying the stock market, you will find shelves of books explaining and advising. This is the age of specialized publications, many of which you never see on your neighborhood newsstand. But the periodicals department of your library can offer samples for your review. If it does not have a specific magazine on hand, inquire if it is available by request. Many libraries participate in consortia, a sharing process that enlarges their capacity through special orders to and from other libraries.

In 1990, 18 national and 26 regional magazines about business and finance were published.[1] Countless financial newsletters are issued each year. Seminars are frequently given on investment opportunities and trends. If a certain publication interests you, say, the newsletter *Personal Finance*, send for a sample copy. Most publications of this type will send a recent issue for a modest fee.

Only a few years ago, few people outside the financial industry could identify the prime rate. Now, when major banks change the interest rate they charge their best customers, it is a top story on the six o'clock news. The most uninitiated people nod knowingly when conversations turn to the national economy.

Rule Number 1:   Begin to Use Resources Now

Utilization of resources is an ongoing opportunity, and many are available at little or no cost. Magazines can help you make many decisions by giving you a chance to increase your technical knowledge and read examples of what others in similar circumstances are doing. Magazines have an advantage over books because of their relatively short lead time. They can present information about changes much sooner than books. A few of the magazines that may interest you include:

- *Barron's*, 200 Liberty St., New York, NY 10028
- *Executive Female*, 127 W. 24th St., New York, NY 10011
- *Forbes*, 60 Fifth Ave., New York, NY 10011
- *Money Maker*, 5705 N. Lincoln Ave., Chicago, IL 60659
- *Changing Times*, Subscription Center, Editors Park, MD 20782

Easy Action List

- Read one new business/investment publication this month.
- Investigate one seminar related to an area of your investment or savings priorities.

**Rule Number 2: Your Good Credit Is a
Valuable Resource**

Although many laws allowing women credit in their own names have been enacted at the federal and state levels, some women feel the credit crunch when they are denied a credit card or loan. The most common reasons for loan refusal are:

1. Bad credit record—bankruptcy, lawsuits, late charges, defaulted loans, and other negative entries in your credit history can work against you.

2. No credit record—the old-fashioned concept, "always pay cash," can backfire when you try to obtain a loan and have no credit standing.

3. Too much debt—monthly payments can devour take-home pay. Most lenders recognize this by adopting a debt ratio formula, which is applied to every application for credit.

These reasons for refusal are formidable, but each can be corrected. It may take time, but the result is worth the effort.

Consider the bad credit record. Some women are saddled with a poor credit record from an errant (and subsequently, absent) husband. Others have had the misfortune of personal bankruptcy. The story that follows illustrates this type of financial devastation.

Wilma R. was a nurse with many years' experience in her profession. Her husband, Karl, was not so settled. He could never find the right job. Finally, to her joy, he located a business he could be enthusiastic about. He and a partner, Sam, would produce and sell custom-made furniture. Karl always had a knack for building things, and Sam had a gift of gab. Wilma withdrew her savings to help finance the venture. She was delighted that Karl had found his niche, and went about her job as usual. All went well for a while, but the partners didn't get along. Sam left town, and it was then discovered that he had been draining the firm of its assets. Wilma was found to be legally liable for the firm's debts and was forced into bankruptcy. It took her several years to work her way out of the financial and emotional abyss.

"The hardest thing about the ordeal was doing without a credit card," she said. "Everywhere you go a credit card is important." The use of the card when checking in at a hotel or as identification were two examples she cited. She studied the laws in her state and recovered slowly.

The "always pay cash or don't buy it" rule may work as a disadvantage when you need a credit record. This can be corrected by deliberately establishing credit. Begin small, and build one prompt payoff upon another. A pay-cash formula need not be abandoned, just modified to allow for the development of a paper trail of good credit.

The high debt ratio can be slowly controlled through self-discipline. When you pay off the easiest debt first, the one with the lowest balance, you will have the satisfaction of seeing tangible progress. The best debt to retire first may be the one with the highest interest rate, rather than the lowest balance. You decide which is best for you. Take part, or all, of the former payment and set it aside for savings or investment purposes. The exercise that follows will show you how to calculate your debt ratio.

How to Calculate Your Debt Ratio

List monthly debt payments:

Car payment(s)	_____
Credit cards	_____
Loans	_____
Other payments you make	_____
Total payments	_____

Divide your monthly take-home pay into the total of your monthly payments. The answer is your debt ratio. For example:

If your debts are $800 and your take-home pay is $2800:

800 ÷ 2800 = .2857, or 28.57%, rounded up to 28.6%, a very high ratio

If the total of your payments is around 10 percent, you are still in the safety zone, but 15 percent is borderline, and 20 percent is a danger sign. Any ratio over the borderline calls for a plan to get better control of finances. Lending institutions always have a ceiling. Inquire what it is.

A hidden factor can work against you here. If you are setting aside tax-deferred savings or any other savings through payroll deduction that reduces your take-home pay, the lending institution *will not count* that savings portion when calculating your ratio, even though you could increase your net pay by a stroke of the pen. Some may not count it even if you are saving at that same institution.

Another method of building credit is through the secured credit card. For women with a poor credit record, or those who have no established record in their own name, this type of card is available—for a price. Essentially, you deposit a stated amount with a bank, usually several hundred dollars. The bank then issues you a credit card with the limit equal to or less than your deposit. Your money on deposit is "locked" in, perhaps earning a small amount of interest. The credit card looks like any other card; only you and the bank know of the secured arrangement. Your next step is to carefully charge small amounts and repay the amount promptly. When opening such an account, inquire whether you can convert to an unsecured credit card after a certain time period and under what circumstances the bank would seize your security savings.

A valuable resource for credit card information is the consumer group Bankcard Holders of America, 460 Spring Park Place, Suite 1000, Herndon, VA 22070. For three dollars, they will send you a list of banks throughout the United States that offer the lowest finance charges on credit cards, and a list of cards with low or no annual fees. You might consider membership in the organization, which qualifies you for these lists free, plus a regular newsletter about credit and related subjects, all for $18 per year.

You may want to know what is in your credit record. It is not difficult to obtain a copy of your file. You should contact a local credit reporting company, or one of the three national agencies. They are Equifax, TRW Inc., and Trans-Union Credit Information Co. Consult your telephone directory yellow pages under "Credit Reporting Agencies." A fee of around $15 is usually charged for this service, unless you have been denied credit. In that case, the report is free and must be sent to you upon your request within 30 days. The report will show your credit history, including late payments and closed accounts. It will also show who has asked to see the report.

The prudent manager will review her credit report every five years or so, to make sure no errors have been made. If an inaccuracy is found, you can ask the credit bureau to investigate. If the issue is not resolved, you may write an explanation to be included with the file. The agency will give you the federal regulations regarding the time lines for these problems. According to *The Wall Street Journal* article entitled "It Can Pay to Peek at Your Credit Report" (Jan. 9, 1990), less than one-half percent of the nine million annual requests for credit files show any error.

Rule Number 3:   Seek Information

As you have developed goals for later years, you have at the same time focused on issues that bear watching. Fortunately, others are doing the same thing, and will share information with you, often at low cost. For example:

- American Association of Homes for the Aging
  1129 20th Street, N.W., Suite 400
  Washington, DC 20036

- Displaced Homemakers Network
  1411 K Street, N.W., Suite 1411
  Washington, DC 20005

- National Commission of Working Women
  1325 G Street, N.W., Lower Level
  Washington, DC 20005

- National Gray Panthers
  806 15th Street, N.W., Suite 430
  Washington, DC 20005

- Older Women's League (OWL)
  730 11th St., N.W.
  Washington, DC 20001

Write and ask for information and any publications they have available, or for their catalog of publications and services.

One organization that stands out for its work on behalf of older people is the American Association of Retired Persons (AARP). Membership is open to people age 50 and up, and the dues are only five dollars per year. Some AARP programs include Widowed Persons Service, Tax Aide, 55 Alive driving program, Women's Financial Information Program and AARP Works employment planning program. AARP has a Women's Initiative which works to ensure that the economic, social health and long-term care needs of midlife and older women are met. Some of their publications include:

- *Coping and Caring*—for the families and friends of Alzheimer's disease patients (D12441)
- *Miles Away and Still Caring*—for those concerned about relatives living at a distance (D12748)
- *Five Ways to Cut Your Phone Costs* (D12175)
- *Insurance Checklist* (D1032)
- *Money Matters*—How to talk to and select lawyers, financial planners, tax preparers, and real estate brokers (D12380)
- How To (series of six folders):
  —Conduct a Security Survey (D396)
  —Protect You and Your Car (D393)
  —Protect You and Your Home (D395)
  —Protect Your Neighborhood (D397)
  —Spot a Con Artist (D394)
  —Protect Your Rural Homestead (D12244)

- *Healthy Questions*—to help you select a healthcare professional (D12094)

- *Protect Yourself—A Woman's Guide to Pension Rights* (D12258)
- *Divorce after 50—Challenges and Choices* (D12909)
- *A Primer on Financial Management for Midlife and Older Women* (D13183)

For a single free copy of these publications, send request with the the title and stock number to: AARP Fulfillment, 1909 K Street, N.W., Washington, DC 20049. Use the number in parentheses after each title when ordering. Allow 6–8 weeks for delivery.

Rule Number 4:   Have Fun, Too

Not all the resources for retirement are serious; some are for fun, such as Elderhostel. Elderhostel provides economical educational programs in more than 1200 institutions in more than 40 countries—all for persons age 60 and above. In 1988, more than 15,000 hostelers attended the overseas programs alone.

A typical program in North America is a week-long stay at a college or university, where participants study, learn, and do. Costs are held down through accommodations at dormitories or hostels.

Carefully detailed course descriptions outline facilities. The courses are generally in the liberal arts and sciences. No exams, grades, or homework are required, with the exception of Intensive Studies, which may include reading assignments. No credits are given for the work. No previous study or knowledge is required. It is not necessary to have a high school diploma, much less college work, to attend.

Most programs in the United States cost $225 per week per person, which includes registration, six nights accommodations, all meals, five days of classes, and assorted extra activities. The cost includes *everything* except transportation. In Canada, the cost is $245 per week per person.

Tall, slender Elaine had a country woman look— tweed skirt, cardigan, and walking shoes. Her brown hair showed very little gray; it was straight and stylish. She was tan, a badge of her devotion to her garden. When she spoke, traces of an English accent came through. She was a psychologist. She said, "The smartest thing I did to prepare for my retirement happened almost accidentally. When I was looking for a house to buy, I found a wonderful Victorian place. On the same property was a cottage, which serves as a source of income now. Better yet, it means that someone will be living close to me when I am older, and I'll be able to remain independent as long as possible."

Since the aim of Elderhostel is to provide a stimulating and intellectual environment in simple accommodations at low cost, shared housing is likely to be offered. Dormitories are not like hotels or other commercial facilities; participants must often be willing to share rooms and bathrooms. Details are carefully described in the organization's materials. A sample of programs might include:

- Art History: Impressionism
- Coastal Wetlands: Birds and Marine Life
- The Shaker Experience
- Peace—More Than the End of War
- Gettysburg in Fact and Fiction

Jack and Gail P. have gone to three Elderhostels and enjoyed every one of them. He was reluctant to go at first, but when he found that he did not have to attend every class, and that there would be many other men there also, he went. He considered his most unusual experience the class on ballet. "I went there to learn about ballet, not to *do* ballet," he laughed. Gail nodded, "He was pretty good, too." They will be going again next summer to study marine life, folk art and the plants of the seashore.

For further information, contact: Elderhostel, 80 Boylston St., Suite 400, Boston, MA 02116.

A quick review of the yellow pages of your telephone directory under "Senior Citizen Service Organizations" may reveal a number of resources you did not know existed. If you are in or near a large city, the list of resources should be long, but smaller cities have more than you may expect. The Los Angeles directory has many entries, including the Los Angeles Council of Careers for Older Americans, the National Council of the Aging, and many ethnic and church-related senior centers. Your local park district, community college, and YMCA/YWCA are all likely to have programs and classes geared to adults and seniors.

Automobile club membership offers the convenience of roadside service in emergencies, as well as travel services and insurance. A review of their material will be worthwhile. Check the white pages of your phone directory and call them to find out what benefits and services they offer their members.

Rule Number 5: Meet With Others

An immediate resource of value is the Women's Network concept. Networks have sprung up throughout the country. Mainly unaffiliated with other organizations, they represent a grass-roots response to women's desire to help one another. Few requirements are needed to join, and the emphasis is on becoming acquainted, forming new friendships and business links. Watch your local newspaper for information about a network in your area. Call the Chamber of Commerce to ask for information.

Service clubs and business organizations are other resources you can develop now. Quota, Zonta, Altrusa, and Soroptomist are women's service clubs where you can network and contribute to philanthropic projects at the same time. Quota Club International, Inc., for example, specializes in helping the hearing- and speech-impaired. Its address, for further information, is 1420 21st Street, N.W., Washington, DC 20036.

In many locations, men's service clubs are opening their doors to women. Some private men's club are now admitting women also. Evaluate the clubs available to you and select one or two that will enhance your career and provide contacts for use later on. Ask businesswomen and church leaders what organizations they belong to and why. When you find one that sounds good, ask to come as a guest. Almost every organization is looking for new members. Shop around.

Rule Number 6: Cost Savings for Retirees and You

Travel interests almost everyone, but the realities of away-from-home costs can be a surprise. Hotel and motel chains have been quick to recognize the growing market of older persons, however, and to offer them and others special benefits. Many chains now offer frequent guest programs, which are available to everyone, as well as senior discounts to persons over a certain age, usually 62 or 65. They will also offer the same discount to persons who are AARP members, even if they don't neet the age requirement. Inquire at the hotel of your choice about any special programs they may have. It is in their best interest to have such a plan—it guarantees them, and members of the same chain, customer loyalty.

Watch the travel section of newspapers for special plans. Travel magazines often feature articles on special locations. Several newsletters are published for travelers, with many good travel tips and special offers included in their articles. Two of these are

- *The Mature Traveler*, Travel Bonanzas for 49ers Plus, P.O. Box 50820, Reno, NV 89513. Subscription rate: $23.50 per year.
- *Consumer Reports Travel Letter*, Box 53629, Boulder, CO 80322-3629. Subscription rate: $37 per year.

Economic conditions may bring changes in discount plans over time, but a few examples of present offers include:

- Hyatt Gold Passport, which gives points for dollars spent in their hotels. The points convert to room upgrades or free stays. Write to Hyatt Gold Passport, P.O. Box 44102, Jacksonville, FL 32231, for more information, or call 1-800-544-9288.
- Worldperks, an example of cooperation among airlines, hotels and car rental services. Dollars spent with Northwest Airlines, National Car Rental, Radisson Hotels, or many others in the program, earn credit to be applied toward airline tickets, room upgrades, and other awards. Write Worldperks Service Center MS:C 6330, Northwest Airlines, Minneapolis/St. Paul International Airport, St. Paul, MN 55111.

Motel chains offer plans, also. The Vagabond Inns in California, Nevada, and Arizona, have Club 55 in conjunction with Nendels in Oregon and Sandman Hotels and Inns in Washington. Special discount rates apply, and a newsletter gives information about specially planned trips for club members. Persons 55 or over are invited to join for a modest $10 one-time fee. For further details, write Vagabond

Inns Club 55, Box 85011, San Diego, CA 92138, or call 1-800-522-1555. Membership comes with a 30-day money-back guarantee.

Individual hotels also may offer specials, such as a discount for retired persons, persons over a specified age, or members of a nationally recognized seniors' organization, such as AARP. Inquire as you make your reservations; do not wait until checkout time and then expect a discount.

Your travel agent will also have information about special rates. In most cases, the client is not charged when a travel agent books tickets and lodging. The agent makes money on commissions from the hotels and airlines. Ask your agent about rates for the off-season or shoulder season, which is the in-between time. Almost every vacation and resort facility has less crowded times. Even if you have a good income and can afford to travel during the peak season, you should consider alternating vacations between peak and shoulder seasons, and putting the savings into your investment account. The shoulder season may even please you more, because it is likely to be less crowded.

Have you thought of leading a tour or helping a tour leader? A significant reduction in your cost, sometimes the entire amount, is your pay. Ask your travel agent or a college extension program that offers excursions for details.

Travel bargains are not the only way to save; you'll discover plenty of others as saving becomes one of your goals. Many of the savings opportunities described here may be used before retirement. Use this new money to reduce debt and thereby provide more savings. Nest-egg and investment portfolio growth can become your hobby—you can spend your time and energy building your fortune.

Using resources will pay a twofold dividend: you have the advantage of their benefits now, and you will have the benefits of their advantages in later years.

Endnotes

1. Neff, Glenda Tennant, ed. *1990 Writer's Market: Where and How to Sell What You Write* (Cincinnati, Ohio: Writer's Digest Books, 1990), pp. 265–270.

Planning Chart—Chapter 13

Your age now:

20s	30s	40s	50s
Begin community activities	Expand activities	Evaluate activities	Evaluate activities
Develop reading habits	Expand and enjoy	Expand and enjoy	Expand and enjoy

Women Helping Women
—The Ultimate Harmony

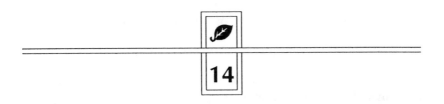

14

Who will take care of women in their later years?

After age 70, only 6 percent of American women are married, even though 95 percent of women living today have been married at some time in their lives.[1]

One study found that among most older parents (80 percent of all people over age 65), more than 90 percent had seen at least one child once or more during the week of the survey. The bonds between children and parents are very strong, and the relationship endures despite any differences the parties may have.[2]

About one-half of persons over age 65 are great-grandparents. Thus, a family structure contains three sets of parents, two sets of grand-parents and grandchildren, three sets of children, and two sets of double-role members who are both parents and children.[3] For the first time in history, the average married couple has more parents than children.[4]

The oldest members of a family are likely to be women because they outlive their husbands by seven to eight years. Older men are almost always married; their care and support comes from their wives, an *intra*generational system. Women, on the other hand, are likely to be alone in their old age, and must draw support from younger people, an *inter*generational system.[5]

Considerable research substantiates that women take the major responsibility for the maintenance of family relationships, including their in-laws. Eight out of 10 older parents living with a child are women, and two-thirds of them live with a daughter.[6]

The burden falls upon women to care for women.

The relationship between grandparents and grandchildren is usually coordinated by the middle generation, the parents, and the woman is again the key player. Divorce can disturb and interrupt contacts between older and younger generations. When this happens older people become isolated and deprived of the opportunity to develop an important support system.[7]

Easy Action List

- Call or write one relative you have not seen recently; do it this week.
- Send a card to a younger family member—for no special occasion, just because you care.

The trend is away from family dependence and toward friends. In one survey of middle-class women ranging from young to elderly, only 25 percent named relatives as close friends.[8] Aside from younger family members, who can an older woman turn to? Her friends will be her greatest resource.

Friendships beyond the most casual contact do not occur without conscious effort. If you want a friend, you must make the effort to be a friend, and exhibit those characteristics that make your friendship valuable. Women are now able to meet prospective friends in many areas, where in the past they had little or no access. Once limited to relatives, church, and neighborhood, they now meet and interact with people:

- on the job and in job-related activities;
- through common interest activities, such as sports, hobbies or cards;
- at classes;
- at child-care centers or children's school activities;
- through friends of their husbands, children, or other friends;
- by working on political campaigns or for popular causes;
- by volunteering and charity work; and
- by joining clubs, lodges, and associations.

Rule Number 1:   Seek New Friends All the Time

The only limitations on choice of friends come from within yourself and your internal selection system. The standards for friendship are formed early in life, and, according to a study by Helen Gouldner and Mary Symons Strong, four elements are active in the process of choosing friends. They are

1. Dislike criteria.
2. Disregard criteria.
3. Liking criteria.
4. Individual budgets for narrowing down candidates.[9]

Dislike criteria are those traits and characteristics that offend us, and for which we have an aversion. Untidiness, dishonesty, and boastfulness might be a few examples. People with these characteristics are usually avoided.

Disregard criteria are those elements we regard as being unsuitable. You may not dislike a person, but you do not like him or her, either, for reasons that are superficial. So you do not pursue friendship with that person.

Liking criteria are the basis for the often demonstrated premise that people choose to be friends with others similar to them. They select people with parallel values and attitudes. They can be expected to have related educational backgrounds, similar intelligence levels, and the same standards. Many studies have demonstrated this.[10]

People with similar tastes tend to congregate in the same locations, thus providing optimal opportunities to develop friendships. The possibility of friendships forming and developing grows as the number and variety of pleasant meetings increases.[11]

Individual budgets for narrowing down candidates refers to the pool of possible friends one might draw upon. Available time, obligations to family, health, and other factors limit choices or the motivation to pursue a friendship. Many of the women in the study had a list of present friends, but also had hopes for future relationships and regrets over lost friendships.[12]

Each woman needs to develop a portfolio of friends, just as she creates an investment portfolio. Almost all women recognize the need to have close women friends, so much so that this type of relationship is almost taken for granted. Close friends transcend mere superficial niceties. A close friend is one you can depend on, especially during times of stress or hardship. Such a friend will listen, give advice and consolation, yet not divulge secrets or confidences. With a close friend you can reveal your innermost thoughts without worry of disclosure. Loyalty, trust, sincerity, and common values are some of the elements important in a friendship. The exercise below may help you discover the traits you value most in a friend.

Network Development Exercise

List your closest friends and their most likable characteristics

1. _____

2. _____

3. _____

List three candidates for becoming close friends

1. _____
2. _____
3. _____

For each candidate, list three ways you will reach out to that person in the next month to become a closer friend

1. _____
2. _____
3. _____

Easy Action List

- Meet this week with one friend you have not seen for a year or more.
- At the next group meeting you attend, speak to one new woman; find out what her hobbies are.

Like the stocks in an investment portfolio, friendships must be monitored and cared for. If the price of a stock falls below a predetermined level, it is best to sell. If a relationship is all one-sided, or if the other person seems to have moved on to other connections and interests, it may be wise to let go and move on to new relationships.

Geographical separations can sometimes cool a friendship, causing you to realize you may not have as much in common as you thought. Divorce or other personal crises may interfere. If a friendship fails or falls away, seek a new friend. No one can be replaced precisely, but new people can bring new interests into your life.

Opportunities in making friends may be common, some can be avoided, as shown in the stories that follow.

Phyllis A. and Joan R. were friends. They worked at the same insurance company, although in different departments. Phyllis was the talkative one, always asking questions about Joan and her family, and talking about others. After a time, Joan noticed that while Phyllis always wanted to know the details of everyone else's life, she said little of her own or of her children. Joan had invited Phyllis to her home for dinners and parties many times, yet Phyllis had never reciprocated. Joan had never seen the inside of Phyllis' house.

Finally, Joan came to the conclusion that the relationship was too one-sided, that she was giving but not receiving. When Joan had a chance to transfer to the company's main office, she let the contact with Phyllis slip away. It was painful for her, but she was not comfortable continuing the relationship on the current basis. She tried to tell Phyllis about her feelings, but Phyllis laughed it off. It was time to end the relationship at that level. They continued to correspond, but at longer and longer intervals. Finally, they lost touch.

Joy D. was a loner. She never joined clubs, and her few friends were all her own age. Her family was small, and she outlived her friends and her generation in the family. It fell upon her only daughter to care for her; there was no one else. Joy had no network. Unfortunately, her declining years were marred by many debilitating strokes, and her poor health and subsequent need for 24-hour care came at a time when her daughter was newly widowed. A friendship network would have saved both women much heartache and stress.

Another important advantage of having a network of friends and supporters of all ages is it helps you remain independent as long as possible. Friends can provide you with the little courtesies and conveniences that will keep your morale and independence intact.

Rule Number 2: Evaluate Your Friendships Honestly

Not all friendships are perfect, and most women overlook weaknesses in their friends. As long as trust and respect for the other remain intact, minor peculiarities are forgiven.

Friends expect loyalty from their friends; they want their close associates to behave favorably toward them. They do not want severe criticism or ego-damaging attacks. Friends seek approval and support. These characteristics make up healthy friendships and are the fabric of rewarding relationships. To be a close friend to someone is an honor and an accomplishment. It takes much attention and energy, but the returns are worth the effort.

An extension of the friendship experience is mentorship. In the business world, a worker, especially a new manager, often seeks out a mentor. The mentor is usually an older, more experienced member of the organization, who is willing to give the newer person the benefit of his or her knowledge. Many younger women who were looking for rapid advancement on career ladders were aided by one or more mentors.

Rule Number 3: Strengthen Your Network Continuously

A new dimension may be added to the mentorship concept by applying it to women outside the business environment. An older woman can offer support, knowledge, and friendship to a younger woman. The authors have coined a new word to describe this phenomenon: *woman*torship. It simply means women helping women.

Not all womantors will become life-long friends with those they help, but the fact that they are available will open doors and be advantageous to both parties.

Let it be known that you would be glad to serve as a womantor to someone seeking support in your particular line of expertise, whether it be banking or baking, sewing or singing. You do not have to give her the equivalent of a college education. A few moments of attentive listening may bring a comment or two from you that will be just the answer she needs. Not only will you benefit through personal satisfaction but being a womantor is an important method of building a network. It also provides an opportunity to build relationships with women of all ages, reinforcing and balancing your support system. Complete the exercise below to discover more about womantors.

In My Memory, Who Are the Women Who Helped Me?

	Name	What she did for me
1.	_____	_____
2.	_____	_____
3.	_____	_____
4.	_____	_____

Who Are the Women I Might Help Now?

	Name	What I could do
1.	_____	_____
2.	_____	_____
3.	_____	_____
4.	_____	_____

Rule Number 4: Remember Your Friends

One way a woman can honor another is by leaving her something of value in her will. Some women say to themselves, "I don't have very much, so I don't need a will." Many cannot face the fact that they may die someday. Some secretly believe that if a person writes a will, it will somehow hasten her death. Others do not know how to begin. Here are some examples where a will would make a difference.

Example number 1: A woman dies before her husband, contrary to statistics. He remarries; most widowers do remarry. His new wife has children of her own. The second wife and her children may inherit the family possessions of the first wife, instead of their being passed to the children of the first marriage. The first wife could have addressed this in a will.

Example number 2: Women often have best friends with whom they are very close. Research has shown that when men are asked, "Who is your best friend?" they usually reply that their wives are. But women almost always say it is another woman.

A best friend may be a sister, a more distant relative, or an unrelated person. If a woman dies without a will (called dying *intestate*), her sister might not inherit if the deceased woman had a surviving husband or children. Her distant relative might not even qualify under the law, and the unrelated woman certainly would not.

Those who would inherit may not know the value of the deceased person's household, or may not care, but a will can protect everyone's interests. It certainly could have protected Lucinda P.'s special treasure—a mourning bonnet that had belonged to Queen Victoria. Ordinarily, the English royal family is very careful about disposal of possessions. Lucinda's grandmother was seamstress to the Queen, and during a trip from London to Scotland made by the royal entourage, word was received from London that her husband, Lucinda's grandfather, had died. Etiquette was very precise in those days, especially among the court staff.

The new widow was expected to wear mourning immediately, but she had no veil and no way to get one, since they were on a train. The Queen gave Lucinda's grandmother her own bonnet as a gesture of condolence and kindness. It was black, of course, with a tiny ruffle around the face, and a black veil was attached to the top.

Years passed, and the bonnet was now in Lucinda's possession. Her close friend, Alma, was the director of a historical museum. Lucinda promised the bonnet to Alma for the museum. Alma always smiled and said, "When you're done with it, dear."

Lucinda did not make any provision for her promise in her will. She had no children, and had been widowed for many years. Her only relatives were two cousins, who were not close to her.

After Lucinda's death, neighbors described to Alma how the heirs wasted no time in cleaning out Lucinda's house. The things they did not want were thrown on a large bonfire in the back yard. The neighbor particularly noticed one cousin run from the house with a small black hat with a veil attached, and how they laughed as she threw it in the fire.

"I learned my lesson," Alma said with considerable bitterness. "Now, when anyone offers anything for the museum, I accept on the spot."

Example number 3:   Items need not have a great historical or monetary significance to be of value to a close friend.

Doreen and Marie were best friends, but were not related. Each was an only child and considered the other "the sister I never had." Doreen died intestate. Everything went to her husband and children.

Marie asked the younger son if, during the disposition of Doreen's effects, he would choose a personal memento for her.

"It need not be of value, but something personal that she especially liked," was the request.

Doreen's son gave Marie a small locket—and inside she found a picture of herself Doreen had taken when they were in high school thirty years earlier. It is Marie's special treasure.

Amy P. was a spinster with no relatives, but with a host of friends in her town, where she had been an art teacher for many years. In her will, she specified that her students might be given "a spoon, a plate, or a painting" if they asked.

Example number 4:   Division of assets among one's children is sometimes puzzling. Some women divide everything as equally as possible, regardless of the way the children have treated their parents. Others reward those who have been more attentive and caring with a greater share than their siblings. The child who nurses a parent for months or years has earned extra consideration.

Example number 5:   If a woman has lent money to one of her children, what should she do? If the money was truly a loan, and not a gift, and any balance remains unpaid at the time of the mother's death, it is only fair that the outstanding amount be deducted from that child's settlement. Otherwise, the other heirs (children, husband, grandchildren, etc.) suffer a loss due to the depletion of the overall value of the estate.

Example number 6: A woman might consider adding a provision in her will to establish a scholarship at her college or university. It can be done in her name or the name of a special person. If she has enough cash and assets to remember those she loved and to pay debts, she might consider establishing a scholarship or two. A life insurance policy with the estate named as beneficiary would probably provide ample cash to cover necessary dispositions, and provide for a scholarship as well.

You can endow a scholarship for less than you might imagine. Contact the financial aid office of your chosen school for details.

Agnes M. did that and found the minimum for a perpetual scholarship at her local community college was $3,000. Only the interest would be used and the principal would remain untouched. She specified two scholarships in her will, one in her own name for students in the business division, and one in honor of her mother for students in the fine arts division (her mother had been a talented painter). Agnes also requested, when she was making her own final arrangements through the local memorial society, that instead of sending flowers to the memorial service, she wanted friends to be asked to contribute to the scholarships she had established.

Example number 7: If you have a substantial estate and are responsible for the care of a family member, you may want to set up a fund to give that person a lifetime allowance. Keep in mind that a reasonable figure by today's prices may not be sufficient after tomorrow's inflation.

Rule Number 5:   Never Be Without an Up-to-Date Will

Writing a will takes care, and is best done by an attorney. Wills can be written in your own handwriting (called a holographic will), but a will that is professionally prepared is much less likely to be upset in case of a dispute. A few telephone calls to attorneys will determine the cost of preparing a simple will.

Begin by making a list of your assets and how you want them divided. Include everything. Remember, the purpose of a will is to withhold as well as to give.

Consider the person you want to serve as executor. This person will be in charge of settling your estate, paying outstanding bills, collecting any money owed you, and satisfying the laws of your state that your intentions are fulfilled and that all taxes are paid. It should be someone who can deal with everyone in a fair and impartial manner. Name an alternate in case your first choice is unable to serve. Depending on the laws in your state, the executor receives a fee for this service, usually determined by a percentage of the value of your estate. The attorney who assists is also entitled to a fee. Both fees come from the assets of the estate before any distribution to the heirs is made.

Be sure to mention who gets the remainder and residue of your estate—all those things you have not mentioned specifically. Do not be surprised if you miss something in the first draft. Lawyers are used to that frantic phone call that says, "I forgot something!"

One last thing about last words—keep your will up to date. People and situations change. Martha, the secretary for the attorney of one of the authors, once said, "I can hardly wait to see what you want to do when you change your will. You write the most interesting will of any of our clients!"

The three-part preparation formula of a strong financial base, a regular wellness program, and a womantorship network will pay remarkable dividends for you in your retirement years. Begin now to establish a path to a way of life that will be all that you want it to be. Avoid common traps of stereotyped roles and their limitations. Strive to be different, independent, and autonomous. Declare your personal Independence Day. It is today. You, and only you, can create your own future.

Endnotes

1. Lesnoff-Caravaglia, Gari, ed. *The World of the Older Woman: Conflicts and Resolution* (New York: Human Sciences Press, Inc., 1984), p. 31.

2. Ibid., p. 26.

3. Hagestad, Gunheld O. "The Family: Women and Grandparents as Kin-Keepers." In Alan Pifer and Lydia Bronte, eds., *Our Aging Society: Paradox and Promise* (New York: W.W. Norton and Co., 1986), p. 145.

4. Ibid., p. 146.

5. Ibid., p. 147.

6. Ibid., p. 150.

7. Ibid., p. 153.

8. Gouldner, Helen, and Strong, Mary Symons. *Speaking of Friendship: Middle-Class Women and Their Friends* (New York: Greenwood Press, 1987), p. 2.

9. Ibid., p. 27.

10. Ibid., p. 36.

11. Ibid., p. 38.

12. Ibid., p. 44.

Planning Chart—Chapter 14

Your age now:

20s	30s	40s	50s
Write your will	Update your will as necessary	Same, also consider setting up a trust	Same
Develop friendships	As friends drop away, develop new ones	Widen your horizons by having friends older and younger than you	Have friendships with women of all ages
Develop network beyond friends and acquaintances	Same	Same	Same

Resources

Employment

Brudney, Juliet F., and Scott, Hilda. *Beyond the Gray Horizon: Job-Keeping* and *Job-Seeking When You Are Over Fifty*. New York: Simon and Schuster, 1988.

Gray, Bonnie; Loeffler, Dorothy; and Cooper, Robin King. *Every Woman Works: A Complete Manual for Women Re-Entering the Job Market or Changing Jobs*. Belmont, California: Lifetime Learning Publications, 1983.

Scollard, Jeanette B. *The Self-Employed Woman: How to Start Your Own Business and Gain Control of Your Life*. New York: Simon and Schuster, 1985.

Employment Support Center
900 Massachusetts Ave., N.W., Room 444
Washington, DC 20001

National Center for Women and Retirement Research
Employment and Retirement Issues for Women
PREP Project
Long Island University
Southhampton Campus, New York.

National Commission on Working Women
1325 G St., N.W.
Washington, DC 20049

9 to 5 National Association of Working Women
614 Superior Ave., N.W.
Cleveland, OH 44113

Prime Time Productivity
National Council on the Aging
600 Maryland Ave., S.W., West Wing 100
Washington, DC 20024

Worker's Equity

American Association of Retired Persons
1909 K St., N.W.
Washington, DC 20049

Financial

Buchanan, Annette, and Weaver, Peter. *What to Do with What You've Got*. Washington, DC: AARP, 1984.

Hirsch, Michael D. *Multifund Investing*: Dow Jones-Irwin, 1987.

Lehmann, Michael B. *The Dow Jones-Irwin Guide to Using* The Wall Street Journal. Homewood, Illinois: Dow Jones-Irwin, 1987.

Sivard, Bonnie. *The Working Woman's Financial Advisor*. New York: Warner Books, Inc., 1987.

Wyse, Lois. *The Six-Figure Woman*. New York: Simon and Schuster, 1983.

Bankcard Holders of America
460 Spring Park Place, Suite 1000
Herndon, VA 22070

Personal Finance Newsletter
P.O. Box 1466
Alexandria ,VA 22313-2062

General Interests and Services

Beattie, Melody. *Co-Dependent No More*. New York: Harper & Row, 1987.

Branden, Nathaniel. *How to Raise Your Self-Esteem*. New York: Bantam Books, 1987.

_____ . *Honoring the Self*. Los Angeles: Jeremy Tarcher, Inc., 1983.

_____ . *If You Could Hear What I Cannot Say*. New York: Bantam Books, 1983.

Doress, Paula Brown. *Ourselves, Growing Older: Women Aging with Knowledge and Power*. New York: Simon and Schuster, 1987.

James, Jennifer. *Women and the Blues*. New York: Harper & Row, 1988.

Levin, Norma Jean. *How to Care for Your Parents: A Handbook for Adult Children*. New York: McGraw-Hill, 1981.

Loewinsohn, Ruth. *Survival Handbook for Widows*. Glenview, Ill.: Scott, Foresman & Co., 1986.

Seskin, Jane. *Alone but Not Lonely: Independent Living for Women over Fifty*. Glenview, Ill.: Scott, Foresman & Co. and AARP, 1986.

Sherman, Charles. *Practical Divorce Solutions*. California: Nolo Press, 1988.

Shields, Laurie. *Displaced Homemakers: Organizing for a New Life*. New York: McGraw-Hill, 1981.

Stearns, Ann Kaiser. *Living Through Personal Crisis*. New York: Ballantine Books, 1984.

Stoddard, Alexandra. *Living a Beautiful Life*. New York: Avon Books, 1986.

_____ . *Living Beautifully Together*. New York: Doubleday, 1989.

American Association of Homes for the Aging
1129 20th St., N.W.
Washington, DC 20036

American Association of Retired Persons
1909 K St., N.W.
Washington, DC 20049

Children of Aging Parents, Inc. (CAPS)
2761 Trenton Rd.
Levittown, PA 19058

Quota Club International, Inc.
1420 21st St., N.W.
Washington, DC 20036

Shared Housing Resource Center
6344 Greene St.
Philadelphia, PA 19144

Health

American Heart Association Publications

—*Dining Out: A Guide to Restaurant Dining*

—*Nutrition Labeling: Food Selection Hints for Fat-Controlled Meals*

—*Heart-Healthy Lunch and Snack Ideas*

—*The American Heart Association Diet: An Eating Plan for Healthy Americans*

—*Walking for a Healthy Heart*

—*"E" Is for Exercise*

—*Rationale of the Diet-Heart Statement of the American Heart Association: Report on Nutrition Committee*

—*Dietary Guidelines for Healthy American Adults: A Statement for Physicians and Health Professionals by the Nutrition Committee, American Heart Association*

Cooper, Kenneth, M.D. *Aerobics for Today's Women*. New York: Bantam Books, 1988.

Lapp'e, Frances Moore. *Diet for a Small Planet*. New York: Ballantine, 1982.

Prevention's Guide to Looking Fit and Fabulous at Forty Plus. Emmaus, Pa.: Rodale Press, 1987.

Stutman, Fred A., M.D., and Africano, L. *The Doctor's Walking Book*. New York: Ballantine, 1984.

University of California, Berkeley, Wellness Letter.
Subscription Department
P.O. Box 10922
Des Moines, IA 50340

Magazines

Changing Times
Subscription Center
Editors Park, MD 20782

Chatelaine
777 Bay St.
Toronto, Ont. M5W 1A7, Canada

Country Woman
Box 643
Milwaukee, WI 53210

Lear's
505 Park Ave.
New York, NY 10022

McCall's
230 Park Ave.
New York, NY 10169

New Woman
215 Lexington Ave.
New York, NY 10016

Redbook
224 West 57th St.
New York, NY 10019

Savvy
3 Park Ave.
New York, NY 10016

Self
350 Madison Ave.
New York, NY 10017

Woman
350 Madison Ave.
New York, NY 10017

Woman's Day
1515 Broadway
New York, NY 10036

Woman's World
270 Sylvan Ave.
Englewood Cliffs, NJ 07632

Working Mother
230 Park Ave.
New York, NY 10169

Working Woman
342 Madison Ave.
New York, NY 10173

Pensions and Retirement Plans

Pension Rights Center, *Directory of Pension Assistance Resources*, Washington, DC

Pension Benefit Guaranty Corporation
2020 K St., N.W.
Washington, DC 20006-1806

Women's Pension Project
918 16th St., N.W.
Washington, DC 20006

Travel

Consumer Reports Travel Letter
Box 53626
Boulder, CO 80322-3629

Elderhostel
80 Boylston St., Suite 400
Boston, MA 02116

The Mature Traveler
P.O. Box 50820
Reno, NV 89513

Vagabond Inn Club 55
Box 85011
San Diego, CA 92138

Worldperks Service Center
MS:C6330
Northwest Airlines
Minneapolis/St. Paul International Airport
St. Paul, MN 55111

Women's Issues

Displaced Homemakers' Network 1
411 K St., N.W.
Washington, DC 20005

Ex-Partners of Servicemen/Women of Equity (EX-POSE)
P.O. Box 11191
Alexandria, VA 22312

National Gray Panthers
806 15th St., N.W., Suite 430
Washington, DC 20005

Older Women's League (OWL)
730 11th St., N.W.
Washington, DC 20001

Creating Your Own Future

Deferred compensation plans. *See* Savings plan,
  employer
"Delight Factor" in job satisfaction, 180-82
Diabetes
  Type I (juvenile), 65
  Type II (adult onset, noninsulin-dependent), 65
"Directory of Pension Assistance Resources," 91
Disability insurance
  easy action list, 79
  as investment, 133-34
  need for, 78-79
  purpose of, 79
  uncancelable, 79
Displaced Homemakers Network, 210
Disposable income, relation of age to, 7
Divorce, impact on retirement savings of, 5
Doctor
  comparing prices for your, 80
  speaking up to your, 62-63
Dollar cost averaging, 158-60
Dollar Cost Averaging Worksheet, 160
Domestic services, Social Security rules for, 16
"Double dipping rule," 94
Drugs, prescription
  comparison shopping for, 63
  easy action list, 63
  generic, 63
  overmedication with, 62
Dying intestate, 227

E

Earning level, women's, 2
Eating habits
  to avoid fatigue and burnout, 125
  easy action list, 64
  tracking, 64-65
Education and retraining for retirees, 177
Elderhostel programs, 60, 212, 214
Elizabethan Poor Laws, 36
Emergency fund, 81-82, 133-34
Employee Retirement Income Security Act of
  1974 (ERISA), 89, 92, 99
Employment
  after retirement, advantages of, 4, 175
  break in service for, 93
  resources, 233-34
Equifax, 210
ERISA, 89, 92, 99
Estrogen, bone mass and replacement of, 66
Exercise program, 60-62
  arthritis process slowed by, 68
  to avoid fatigue and burnout, 125
  easy action list, 62
  osteoporosis and, 66, 68
Expense worksheets, 45, 48
  annual, 51
  cash flow, 50
  monthly, 49
Expenses, tracking current, 44-52
  categorization of spending after, 45-46
  sentence stem technique to explore feelings
    about, 45
External power, accepting, 12

F

Family
  income and expense projections, 6
  structure, 219-20
  will provision for care of, 229
  work done by, rules for, 16
Farm workers, Social Security rules for, 16
Fatigue, controlling, 125-26
Federal Deposit Insurance Corporation (FDIC),
  48, 134
Federal employees, Social Security rules for, 16
Federal Savings and Loan Insurance Corporation
  (FSLIC), 48
Finances
  overextending by using credit cards, 54
  resources, 234
  unpreparedness to handle, 39
  woman as full, active partner in, 147-48
Financial goals, 109
  long-term, 115
  medium-term, 115
  near-term, 115
Financial planner
  certified, 141
  easy action list, 141
  fees and charges of, 141-42
  questions to ask, 140
Financial planning notebook. *See* Retirement
  plan
Financial position
  easy action list, 56
  evaluating your current, 39-57
  feelings about current situation with, 41
  projected retirement, worksheet for, 116
Form SSA-7004 (Social Security Administration),
  21, 24
401(k) plan. *See* Savings plan, employer
Fractures, osteoporosis and, 66, 68
Friendships
  easy action list, 223
  evaluating, 224-26
  remembered in your will, 226-29
  seeking, 221-24
Fries, James F., 72

G

Garage sales, saving proceeds from, 123
Goal Progress Chart, 112
Goals
  breaking down major, 108
  determining evaluation method for, 110
  easy action list, 108, 110
  establishing realistic time frame for, 110
  financial. *See* Financial goals
  general areas in which to apply, 109
  giving yourself credit for, 113-15
  for investments, setting, 136-37, 146
  reviewing progress and adjusting strategy to
    achieve, 109, 110
  sentence stem technique for setting, 107-8
  setting concrete, measurable, 109-10
Gouldner, Helen, 221, 231
Government caring for you, myths about, 150
Guthrie, James W., 189

About the Authors

Judith Martindale is a Certified Financial Planner and Registered Investment Advisor. She appears regularly on the "Money Wise" segment of the CBS/KCOY-TV Evening News and can be heard weekdays on local radio. She teaches Family Financial Management for Cuesta College in addition to other financial short courses for adults. Judi manages her financial planning firm in San Luis Obispo, California, through Titan Value Equities, a registered broker/dealer, member SIPC. Judi specializes in financial planning for women.

Mary J. Moses is Director of Personnel of the Office of the San Luis Obispo County Superintendent of Schools. She has long championed women's causes and was the first Affirmative Action Coordinator for Cuesta College. Mary has taught classes on personnel policy procedures. She and Judi have been team teaching since 1982.

For more information regarding workshops, seminars or additional books, please contact:

Sourcebooks, Inc.
P.O. Box 372
Naperville, IL 60566
(708) 961-2161